Naomi Mitchison

The Africans

Panther

Granada Publishing Limited
Published in 1971 by Panther Books Limited
3 Upper James Street, London W1R 4BP

First published by Anthony Blond Limited 1970
Copyright © Naomi Mitchison 1970

Acknowledgment: The map 'How Africa Should be Divided'
from *Sir Harry Johnston and the Struggle for Africa* by Roland Oliver,
is reproduced by kind permission of Chatto & Windus Limited,
London

Made and printed in Great Britain by
Richard Clay (The Chaucer Press), Ltd.,
Bungay, Suffolk.
Set in Monotype Baskerville

Naomi Mitchison is a member of the famous Scottish Haldane family. She runs a Highland farm for part of each year, and the remainder of her time is spent in Southern Africa, in Botswana, of which country she is an honorary citizen. She has also, in her long and active life, published over 50 books, mainly historical novels, many of which are bestsellers.

Contents

Maps

Time Charts

FOREWORD

I began writing this book in the Tribal Office of the Bakgatla in Mochudi. I am doing some of the copious revising that such books need, in the same place, though it is now called the District Office. This was in the Bechuanaland Protectorate, now independent Botswana. I am a member of the tribe, a Mokgatla; it would be unthinkable to suppose that my friends who work in the office or come in and out are in any way different from me because their skins are darker than mine, and their hair curls crisp and close to the head.

We talk a lot about history and I have done some teaching as well. I have plenty of reference books and I have read widely in libraries, as well as looking at things and talking with historians, but most of the older books at least are written from a point of view which begins to make me uneasy. I am still more uneasy when I see the kind of textbooks they read in the schools. They are not, to my mind, adequate reading for young Africans who must be aware of their own history, must judge it fairly, and must feel that there is matter for great pride in it. Today, far too many think that it all began with the coming of the whites and that nobody else matters. Yet that, on the whole, is how they would feel after reading the version of history which is presented to them, and which makes them less able to think for themselves and take responsibility.

That is why I am trying to write their African background history from an inside Africa point of view.

There is a special reason why I can do it. I come of a great Scottish family, the Haldanes, who have known, encouraged and accepted great changes. Even in my own lifetime there has been change from a society based strictly on class in which my family were near the top, to something approaching classlessness. But also I have considerable experience of the Highlands and of fairly recent Highland history, including the destruction of the clan system. There are many analogies between Highland and African people and history; I think these may be helpful and illuminating so they will be found in several places in this book.

It seems to me essential that peoples in different parts of Africa should know how the rest were living during the African Past. This means that in choosing the facts that I have used for this book, I have an African audience in mind, although I hope also that it will help people in Great Britain to understand more about this continent. It is impossible to put in all the facts about any situation. Writers of history inevitably choose the facts and make the comments on them which fit their historical thesis; it is better to be aware of this than not to know what one is doing. But if I am biased in a pro-African way, I do not think that I have ever so far forgotten myself as to have invented evidence or told deliberate lies. If I had done that I would have been shamed before the gentle and truthful people of my tribe.

Outside the Office is *kgotla,* the Chief's court, a space that will hold several thousand people if they pack close, as I have often seen them, and at the back a solidly built shelter of dark branches, where cases can be tried, with a view to restoring the moral order of the tribe. There are always people sitting around, discussing. The Chief—Kgosi—slender, long-legged, perhaps, wearing a bright shirt and shorts, moves between office and *kgotla,* or maybe comes to me for a moment's consultation. His job is to get the whole tribe into the technological future, without losing some essential African-ness, which he sometimes sees clearly, but which sometimes eludes and puzzles him. He knows that if he goes on acting as an old-fashioned chief, which is what some—perhaps most— of his people would like him to do, he will stay in the past, and the future, which goes with ballot boxes and political parties, will overwhelm him and then his people would be desperately hurt, even if they did not realise it at once. I think he is too intelligent and too full of political idealism to let that happen; I think he is trying to lead his people towards democracy, towards the taking over of his own power, though not yet of all his responsibilities. I hope he may be one of those who will shape yet another of the many versions of democracy; I think it may be based on the African concept of the moral order.

He will have to move fast, with thought and courage and generosity, into a future which neither he nor I can foresee. Perhaps he will not be able to get there in time, but every attempt is part of history; the thrown stone cannot but spread its rings. It is possible that here, in Botswana, it may be a genuinely non-racial future; it is not that yet. But if it comes, I think Kgosi and those who go with him into the future will have forgiven and laughed at a hundred little insults and will perhaps remember how one white, their mother, sitting in the office with her type-writer, loved them and tried to help and work for them and encourage them to think and work for themselves. If any con-clusions or bias in this book anger those who have been brought up with another view of history, remember it was written, not out of hate, but out of love.

One

The Wanderers

Let us look at Africa, first of all the size of the continent. It is about 5,000 miles long, with a mainland area of over eleven million square miles; the Nile is over 4,000 miles long, the Niger 2,600 miles, the Congo almost 3,000 miles. It is BIG.

When one begins to ask how many people live there, it becomes more difficult. Census figures usually underestimate, partly because country people all the world over are suspicious of being numbered, partly because some of them still live in deep forest or wander with cattle and may just not be anywhere in particular on census day. But it looks as though the total population of Africa may be somewhere between 280 and 300 millions. That is not a very large figure, and the sub-continent of India, for instance, has nearly twice the number of people living in it. But if one breaks down the figures, one finds that most of the millions are concentrated in the most fertile areas. Nigeria, for instance, counted as a whole, has perhaps 50 to 55 millions, though even this does not equal the crowded population of Great Britain. Uganda has only seven million, Zambia three-and-a-half.

If we break these figures down further, we might, for instance, knock off 50 millions for the countries round the Mediterranean which are all fertile; the Nile valley and delta is one of the most densely populated areas in the world. These countries are not part of Negro Africa; they are different in ethnic grouping, in political and economic interests, and sometimes in social and religious outlook. But they cannot be left out of African history.

Out of the remaining 230 to 250 millions, there are less than four million Europeans. Of these, three million are in the

Republic of South Africa. There are under half a million Indians
and Arabs. But of course if we counted the Mediterranean countries there would be many more Europeans and Arabs.

This gives us an idea about the number of people whose history
this book will try to tell. There is room for more people in Africa,
but only if they can be fed properly and live in conditions toler-
able for human beings. The climate of Africa is violent and this
has kept people poor. Sudden storms leach the soil; even in areas

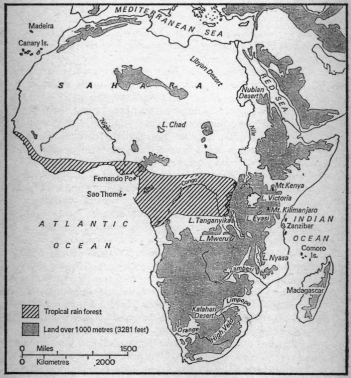

Map 1.

of heavy leaf fall the humus content of the soil is only an eighth that of reasonably good soils in Europe and North America. In one African country all the mealies and corn are withered by drought and people are starving. But, little more than an hour's flight away, some river has flooded out for miles and miles, and there too people have lost their crops and homes.

There are huge areas where there are no people living. Some of these areas are too dry, for instance the Sahara, the Libyan and Nubian deserts and, in most years, the Kalahari. Some are infested with tsetse flies which carry dangerous illnesses for both people and cattle. There is still malaria and various dangerous fevers; there is bilharzia weakening whole populations. In some parts of Africa agriculture, ranching and even game ranching would not be possible with the best present-day techniques. Yet we must ask ourselves whether these areas could be made habitable if money, effort and scientific knowledge were put to work as they are, for example, in the development of nuclear missiles and anti-missiles. But before that is done we want to be quite sure that Africans are going to live there, and that any natural resources—minerals and oil as well as the natural fertility of the soil or natural forest—are going to be used by and for them.

Yet as things are it is a good thing that there are still all these uninhabited spaces. In some, if one flies low over them, seeing no signs of people or of domestic animals, one can still see signs of the beautiful and exciting wild beasts of central, eastern and southern Africa. Room must be found for them because so long as men and women need to be rested from the sight of one another and the things which people make—cities, factories, streets— they will want to look at wild animals and they will pay for the privilege, so that elephants and giraffes, buck, hippos and zebras, ostriches and lions or the lovely brilliant birds are a kind of living gold mine, a garden of animals to be loved and cultivated and cropped. The old days of murderous 'sport' by outsiders are almost over, though some people still need to kill game for food and some kinds of wild animals can be 'farmed' for large-scale human consumption. But the future holds more and more for a visitor with a camera and cine-projector. The wild beasts are the first and easiest natural resource out of which the emergent African states can make some revenue. Naturally I am not comparing them in cash value with the very valuable specialised crops of some countries, Ghanaian cocoa, Nigerian palm oil, Tanzanian copra or cashew nuts, nor with the mineral resources of Zambia and Congo. But they must not be left out.

Wild animals have been there for a long time. So here and there have people. But seldom exactly the same as now. People in Great Britain are not much like the Ancient Britons, especially the Britons who were in the country before the Celtic invasions; the British today are a mixture of Briton with Celt, Saxon, Dane, Norman and often other incomers. So it is in Africa. I look around me in the town of Mochudi and see half-a-dozen different types of face. But all are Batswana, that is speakers of one language, Setswana, and all are citizens of Botswana and will in turn perhaps be citizens of an African federation of states which will probably be one stage on the way to the time when we are all citizens of one world.

Where did all these people come from and how do we know about them? The earliest evidence is from archaeology, that is the evidence of bones and tools and pots which can now be accurately dated in several ways to within a few hundred years. It seems by now possible that there are several centres in the world from which races of men developed from a just pre-human stage, all going through long periods of slow development, in using the first tools, bone and stone, learning about fire, inventing some kind of pottery, hafting their first tools on to sticks so as to dig with them, then making spears and arrows, and, above all, wondering how to solve the problems of the natural world around them which seemed so full of enemies and yet gave them all that they lived by. It seems probable that the first to cross the ape-human line lived in Africa. These gradually developing groups ended up as men and women, not separate species but interbreeding and able also to fertilise one another with new ideas and new techniques. It looks as though the remains of definite 'men', hunters and trappers, from the Olduvai gorge in the Rift valley of Kenya date back well over a million years, and may easily have developed there and lived there, so to speak, 'always'. These remains are older than any yet found in Europe or Asia. Probably they were rather short people, more like the modern Bushmen than the modern Negro African.

There is plenty for the archaeologist to find out about Africa and in some ways it will be easier here than in Europe. This is because almost all European land has been so changed and worked over, most of all in the places where early men might have lived, that it has become more and more difficult to find out what happened before the recent changes.

It seems likely that natural selection brought out dark pigmentation as a protection against the ultra-violet rays which in the tropics redden, dry up and line a white skin. European body fur and long hair were equally useful against northern cold and wet. Other physical characteristics gradually worked into the gene structure of the many races of the world. Those most admired in and by the various races are often associated with rather out-of-date pursuits like war and hunting.

What happened to these first people? If we look at a map of Africa we can see that across the middle there is a belt of heavy rainfall with lakes and forests. This extends well to the south, but where the forest thins out, and there is still a reasonable rainfall, there are the conditions for rich grasslands or farming. The people who gradually developed into different groups, speaking different languages, were mostly hunters and collectors of vegetables, roots, fruit and honey, just the same as early people all over the rest of the world. This was rich country giving them all they needed; they wandered about, perhaps rarely meeting people beyond their own extended family group. Long separations produced different sets of words. Neither nature nor other men forced them into cultivation and permanent dwellings. It was only comparatively recently that they took to grazing and herding cattle and very recently, historically speaking, that they took to farming.

North of the heavy rainfall belt, the forest thins out again. Further north there is now desert, but as we shall see, it was not always like that. Then, there is fertile land again along the Mediterranean coast, and, in the north-east, Egypt and the land bridge to south-west Asia and what is generally called the fertile crescent or the cradle of civilisation.

People start by wandering in little groups for thousands of years, first hunting and food-gathering, with no tame animals except hunting dogs and later with flocks and herds. They only settle when they find land that will bear one crop after another without needing the comparatively modern techniques of crop rotation or fertilisers. Shifting cultivation, which usually means coming back every fifteen years or so to the same patch of regenerated soil, is another possibility in land with fairly heavy rainfall where secondary forest (small trees and bushes) comes back quickly after a year or two of cropping and makes new soil, as well as providing wood which can be burnt to help fertility by making potash. But this method cannot support such a large population as other kinds of farming.

Cereal growing was developed first in river valleys where alluvial mud gave the fertility and where there is no erosion problem. What we call civilisation started in these flat river valleys; in the Euphrates plain, on the Indus and the Chinese rivers, on the Nile. A crop is something that gives back more than was sown, three times, even ten times, and the surplus gives people time and energy to build temples and villages, to fortify them, to make themselves cities and the laws that have to exist so as to run the cities properly. History in all parts of the world shows us that people must then satisfy something in themselves which perhaps they cannot even name; they give themselves a top structure of people who do not cultivate the soil, priests and kings for example. But after a time, these non-workers gather to themselves more and more power and wealth, and this has to come in the end from the people who do the work.

Once the first needs, food and shelter, are satisfied, curiosity can begin; people begin to wonder why the corn grows, why the sun rises and the stars swing evenly round. They wonder about death and try to avoid having to accept it. They begin to feel that there are secrets and perhaps these are known to the priests and kings. Meanwhile trade begins, first between town and country. People find they must keep a grip of events and numbers which are too much for human memory; they invent some way of making lists and tables, perhaps a calendar. Suddenly, they have discovered writing and arithmetic. Wandering people have less need for all this. They do not have to have such elaborate rules or laws. They can keep knowledge in their heads. It may be more important to be able to cope with a new situation than to have ways of repeating an old one. The skills they need are the skills that can be set up in a new place and that people can remember; the tools they need can be carried.

In Europe waves of invaders came in from the east and north-east. Some of them are known mostly by legend; for instance, the Dorians who came down into Greece, or the shepherd kings who conquered Egypt. Other invaders came in times and places in which chronicles were being kept; Celts, Saxons, Goths and Visi-Goths, Vandals, Huns. They swept down into Europe, looking immediately for food, but, as they got to know the ropes, increasingly for plunder and conquest. Equally, waves of invaders poured into India and China. In Africa they were not headlong, purposeful marches; people drifted over hundreds or thousands of years, and only settled when things seemed very favourable, not thinking of this settling as being a quite different way of life. There might be lucky combinations. Someone might think of using a barbed spear as a fish harpoon. There might be clay which would make good pots. The same kind of chance may easily have happened in the Neolithic period (before the discovery and use of metal) in the Rift valley of Kenya or along the Thames or the Seine or the Ganges.

Another way of knowing about early people is by pictures. In favourable times art develops, as a kind of glorified play which may be partly purposeful magic. If the artists have the luck to use a durable material, these may last far beyond any other knowledge of the people who made them, as rock paintings have done, some in Europe and many in Africa. The Rhodesian and South African rock paintings still delight the beholder who is willing to accept their stylisation (about as much of an aesthetic effort as appreciation of Picasso); but who made them? It looks as though hunting people started painting these kind of pictures some six thousand years ago and went on until about the time when agriculture took over from hunting; perhaps from the days of bone axes and flint-tipped spears until the days of copper and iron, and even in some places, until a few centuries ago.

But meanwhile the people of the great river valleys, especially Egypt, were developing into the splendid civilisations which we have all heard about. In early times Egypt had many connections with the rest of Africa. It is probable, in fact, that most Egyptians along the upper Nile were as definitely African as, for instance, the people of ancient Numidia or Mauretania before the Carthaginian traders or the Romans came. Yet this never comes into classical history books nor is it mentioned by, say, Herodotus, for whom all non-Greeks were equally barbarian but equally interesting. In the northern delta region of Egypt there was intermarriage as well as social exchange with the many sea-going Mediterranean peoples. It may well be that the heart-land of northern Africa from which the wanderers mostly came, just as other wanderers came into Europe from some heart-land beyond the Caucasus, was the Saharan region. This, as we shall see, was not a desert in early times and it is quite likely that some of the Saharan wanderers came east to the Nile valley and settled there.

Do not let us go too much by looks. There are many kinds of African face and form. A Zulu, a Kikuyu, a Berber or an Ashanti are as different from one another as a Norwegian, an Irishman and a Sicilian in Europe or as a Tamil and a Nepalese in India. An Ethiopian may look rather like an Egyptian or rather like a Ugandan. One country cannot claim to be more African than another.

But the ancient Egyptians, with their wonderful river, which fertilised the corn-growing land every year with the mud left from the slow settling of flood water, probably thought of themselves as being richer and nobler and more powerful than their neighbours, possessed of greater secrets, magic and technology. They sent off constant trading or sometimes conquering expeditions towards their southern neighbours, from the second millenium BC onward. Queen Hatshepsut's proudest moments c. 1480 BC were when her merchant captains came back from their great trading ventures. You can still see the story all set out, splendidly carved in stone on terraces high above the Nile valley. And again, c. 1370 BC in one of the tombs of the nobles there is a fresco of Akhnaton, the first rebel against the power and intolerance of the priesthood, preaching to the multitude. The rays of Aton, the beneficient light, are shining down on him and them, and among the audience, whose heads are thrown back, laughing with delight and liberation, there is one head which is unmistakably middle or southern African.

TIME CHART

1550-1450 BC

Egypt. Queen Hatshepsut sends out expeditions. Egypt in a high degree of civilisation. Medicine being developed. The Book of the Dead written.

Mediterranean. After the earlier disaster the civilisation of Knossos is in full swing. The Mycenaean civilisation also: the Lion Gates. Mycenaean colonists in Spain. The beginnings of Ionian and Achaean invasions and cultures. The Dorian invasion in the north beginning.

Near East. In the Hittite Empire the high priests are dominant and produce impressive art forms. Possible date for Abraham. Trade developed with India and China.

India. Gradual conquest by the northern peoples and withdrawal of Dravidians into the South. Earliest monuments. Sanskrit poetry.

China. The Shang-Yin Dynasty. Walls and temples: bronzes, some pottery. Writing and astronomy start.

Northern Europe. Bronze age cultures: spiral ornaments and brooches. Possibly the Rigveda poems being composed.

Earliest beginnings of Mexican culture.

It was when the Egyptian empire was in decline that the Nubian land of Kush, originally a colony or dependency, became a great power with first Napata and then the city of Meroe as its capital. In turn, Kush invaded Egypt, and ruled there for some three generations, until the Assyrians 'came down like a wolf on the fold' and drove them back, conquering the fertile Nile valley themselves. The remains of the Kushite civilisation leave us with puzzles to solve. It was rich, gold-producing; it had kings and queens, temples and city buildings; it had pottery and written inscriptions. Most important of all, the people smelted iron for implements and weapons. We can still make out the long slag heaps, after two thousand years. It was probably from there that the important technique of iron-working spread throughout Africa; though this is not necessarily so. There may, in the days when the Sahara was not a forbidding desert, have been a spread south from cities such as Carthage. Hannibal's elephants must almost certainly have been Saharan, which makes one wonder why African elephants cannot be tamed today. There must have been plenty of wheat and other cereals in Meroe, with oxen and sheep, to support the life of the city.

Yet some people wandered away from the lands of Kush. Were they traders who just happened to go on and on? Certainly Meroe was a centre of trade routes and had after a time developed

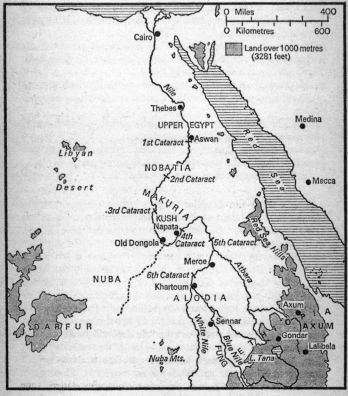

Map 2

its own script for its own language. When scholars at last manage to read this, we may learn more about the slag heaps. Were the wanderers from the Nile valley oppressed by their rulers, or were they younger sons without prospects or did it happen that one year food was short? And what sort of country did they move into? The natural way to go was west into the dipping sun.

We know for certain that the Sahara was not the desert that it is now. The main way we know this is through the Saharan rock paintings. While the painters of southern Africa were busy on their pictures, hundreds more were being painted in rock shelters in the middle of the Sahara. Some are definitely religious or magic pictures, but a great many are just pictures of what was going on. The evidence they produce is startling. Early on, well over three thousand years ago, there must have been a rich country there, not only grazing giraffes, buck and antelope, wild sheep and buffalo, but also rhinoceros, elephants and hippopotami—there is a picture of men in canoes surrounding a hippopotamus, and in the same group of caves, ancient fish bones. All this in the middle of the Sahara! The first set of people in these pictures were hunters; they used spears or bows and arrows; we can get some idea of their gods and their dancing; we know how they decorated themselves; there are even drawings of masks. And we know they were in the second millenium BC. These people were certainly Negroes.

But in the same rock shelters you get evidence of other people coming in, especially cattle herdsmen—there are splendid frescoes of immense herds of cattle. Could over-grazing on top of a climatic change have helped the transformation of the Sahara into dust? Probably not if the cattle were always moving on. But it might have meant overcrowding and a further incentive to people to try living somewhere else. In rather later frescoes there is a distinct Egyptian influence. Someone painted four lovely little bird-headed goddesses—an Egyptian prisoner or trader or someone who had been to Egypt? There are also occasional paintings of huts and women working in the fields, which proves to some extent that people were settled. Insofar as one can tell by their faces, there were several different kinds of African there and some of the pictures show fights between cattle herdsmen and raiders. One exciting thing that is clear from the Saharan frescoes is that these people used war-chariots. These, with their horses, are clearly painted. In the later pictures there are fewer of the large game beasts; perhaps the swamps had already dried up. But at least it was country that people could and did live in and pass through.

Where else did the wanderers come from? We know where Meroe, and Axum, the Ethiopian hill state which succeeded it, finally conquering it about the middle of the fourth century AD, fit into the modern map. We know too that they traded with the Mediterranean and that Axum had quite extensive trade with India and perhaps China. Perhaps some of the wanderers came originally from south-west or even south-east Asia. From there and from Meroe, they carried with them their idea of God and their knowledge of metal working. One way we know this is because of the persistence of certain god forms, especially the ram-headed god, something to do with the thumping, rain-bringing, murdering thunder, which seems to have survived wherever these people went.

But they did not màrch straight on. They did not know where they were going. They did not know of any land boundaries or any distant sea which would stop them in the end. They did not, probably, think of themselves as a nation or part of a nation, though perhaps the Kushites, fleeing with whatever of their household goods they had rescued, after the conquest by the Axumite Ethiopians, remembered the glories and comfort of Meroe. But these grew more and more dream-like as the years went by.

No doubt the wanderers would find empty lands where there was good grazing for their tired flocks and herds. They would stay gathering roots and fruit, hunting, setting up their gods and making a shrine for their sacred objects (think of the lesser wandering of the Israelites), clearing or burning off a piece of land and taking a crop or two before moving on. It seems likely that cereal cultivation was practised in south-west Asia in at any rate the fifth millennium BC. From there the practice gradually spread through Egypt and south to Meroe, and the people who left Meroe around the second and first millenium BC took seed corn with them and sowed it where they stopped for a season. In this way it slowly spread into western Africa, but took longer to reach the southern half. However, cereals are not the only crop; other indigenous plant and root crops were probably being cultivated elsewhere.

Over several thousand years there have been these continuous movings of people, towards what seemed to them to be better conditions. Some of this was doubtless due to changing climates, too much or too little rain. Very thick forest tends to be a barrier and the southward movement may mostly have taken place along the tsetse-free upland ridge of eastern Africa, part of which is the Kenya highlands. Inside the forests people from another source—perhaps originally from the Rift valley—were left comparatively undisturbed until recently, to build up their own relationships with life and the forest. For early movements the evidence is partly in today's languages, physical build, customs and so on, and partly in oral tradition and songs. There is considerable difference of opinion among historians on place of origin and dates, as indeed there is for early European and Asian migrations of peoples.

Probably these wanderers in the part of Africa north of the forest belt, who were on the move three or four thousand years ago, did not go far into the deep forest country, but stayed in the savannahs and open bush where there was enough rainfall for grazing but not terrifying darkness and swamps nor evil beasts and insects. We newcomers going along roads and paths which are constantly being cleared from furiously encroaching vegetation, can afford to see the deep forest as beautiful and exciting; the giant trees whose unseen canopies make the lightless sky, only dropping thick and unexpected blossoms here and there— trees that show from the air as a patch of red or purple among the sea of green—their grey buttress knees hardly visible behind the lower struggle of forest, matted and thorned and dark, and below that again the great leaves veined with colour, hairy or smooth, of the ground plants. No flowers but instead the constant dance of butterflies. I am thinking now of Nigeria; I am thinking of a pool in a forest stream where I swam above spotted and banded fish, among flowering lilies, under the blue gauze wings of dragonflies. But if you are looking for today's and tomorrow's food, if you are unvaccinated, uninoculated against yellow fever, unprotected against malaria, the rain forest may be less beautiful. Many of the food plants which modern Africa knows so well were not introduced until a few centuries ago, long after the wanderers had settled; maize and cassava and the more recent cocoa were yet to come from the Americas, coconuts, bananas, Asian yams and pineapples from Asia or Malaysia, citrus fruit from Asia Minor. Yet gradually people found out— as the ancestors of Europeans and Asians did—what was good to eat, what poisonous and what perhaps had healing properties.

Of course there were far fewer people altogether in Africa than there are now, just as there were far fewer in every part of the world. (It is worth remembering that of all the human beings who have ever existed, almost one in twenty-five are alive now). We do not know for certain what the first Africans looked like. But we have some ideas about one of the main south-western settlements of the wanderers. These are the village people of the 'Nok culture' in northern Nigeria who probably lived between around 300 BC and AD 200. Something of their culture has survived: decorated things, stone tools and terracotta figures, including heads with little beards. They may have had quite complex social and religious systems; they probably had music and dancing. But perhaps we shall never know any more about them.

We do know there were wanderers south of the central forest belt just as there were north of it. In later chapters we shall see something of the movements of the southern Bantu and the displacement of other populations. For thousands of years there must have been meeting and mixing and then gradual separating out again as people began to practice agriculture of some kind and stabilise in centres. Groups might quarrel and fight and probably those with bronze weapons would be able to kill those who had only stone and bone, and later those with iron weapons would conquer the bronze or copper-bearing peoples. But when there is enough room none of that necessarily happens. There can be a mingling of race and speech. Trade is older than conquest; the early Rift valley peoples—so very long ago!—traded their obsidian, which makes steel-sharp knives, for hundreds of miles around. Languages separated or borrowed from one another. But the learned are still arguing vigorously about the relationships between the different groups. Luckily while they do this, the people who speak the languages go on making songs and stories and, increasingly, writing them down.

We can also be certain that the diversity of looks and language groups which was apparent in the very first written records about Africa was already there probably two or three thousand years ago. People had split off into nations or what are often called 'tribes'. This is a word which is used inaccurately, often by politicians or writers, who want to belittle other people and think that the word tribe makes them seem out of date and unprogressive. Anyone who really wants to understand history must keep a careful look-out for inaccurate use of words by politicians who want to make one set of people sound important and civilised and another set unimportant and in some way wicked. See if you can catch me doing this!

Let me now make it clear what I mean by tribe and nation, since I use both words. Anthropologists have defined 'tribe' in various ways; some also use 'clan' for small groups with an authentic common ancestry. We must remember that, during early trading days, Europeans used the words nation and king (or the equivalent in Portuguese, French, etc.) when talking about Africans. But after they had started colonising they used tribe and chief, which lowered the tone of the conquest situation. District Commissioners were careful not to translate the African word as 'king', though on the west coast the local word (*oba*, for example) was used, when king would be the only reasonable translation. Nation was re-invented in Africa quite lately and normally did not apply to the old groupings as such, since the colonialist boundaries, often including such important things as roads, railways and telegraphic or telephonic communications, were now used for the new nation.

When I write 'tribe' I mean a social entity, probably derived from an ancestor figure and his following, but held together by common organisation, customs, laws, language and above all feeling. There is usually, but not always, a head figure or leader, lay or religious in significance, usually a council of some kind with elements of face-to-face democracy, and some kind of welfare service, though often on a level of grinding poverty. Sometimes what is described, for political purposes, as a tribe, is clearly, even in today's world, a nation. Sometimes it is as small as, say, the Scottish nation in the thirteenth century. Sometimes it is little more than a few villages or even, among the rare non-settled peoples, a few families. But it is always cohesive, in a way that a modern nation cannot be except in times of crisis, and thus answers a basic human need.

Several tribes can come together amicably, especially if all speak the same language, and have the same kind of customs; this is a matter of convenience and economy in the modern world, where for certain purposes (but by no means all) a large unit is preferable. It is also of course essential for a modern military machine, if this is thought to be necessary. If all goes well people will develop a national loyalty and friendliness; they will become interested in the workings of the national organisation and in national politics; they will take part and be willing to sacrifice individual good or present well-being for the nation and its future progress; but this love and loyalty will not go as deep as the tribal one, and cannot be induced by suppressing 'tribalism'. Nationalism may be the next step towards an international loyalty to all mankind, though there may be intermediate steps such as African (or European) unity, the danger being that these may be used instead of the real international unity in which alone we can truly have fearlessness and generosity towards all our fellow beings. But it will still remain that for certain kinds of necessary human satisfaction, some smaller organisation must exist, larger than the family. When, as in most of Africa, there is such an organisation, in the form of the tribe, I suggest that the object must be, not to destroy this but to develop it.

Two

The First States

A long, long time and gradually a finding of safe and fertile places, the settling and growing of a way of life : families farming, raising crops, bringing up children, guarding themselves against wild beasts, not thinking very much but going on day to day as country people do all the world over : making up songs and singing them, dancing, carrying water in pots, hunting and trapping, making and improving tools, making and worshipping gods, doing the same things year after year. It is not always easy for us, even with our modern techniques, to date this life. Little is left to see, especially in damp, hot climates where fungus and mould and insects destroy anything within a few years, and the wild bush ramps and tramples with roots and stems breaking up and blotting out walls and floors. Perhaps, too, the earth was kind and fertile and people did not have to invent and struggle. Yet we do know that after a while which nobody measured but which may have been many generations, other invaders came, probably from the same direction as the first, and we know more about them because they had a new kind of organisation which has left more trace, in surviving objects and in travellers' tales. They founded organised states or kingdoms and sometimes these states went on for centuries; we know their names; we begin to know the names of their kings and gods.

The odd thing is that almost all these states show some signs of Egyptian origin. There is always a god-king, half hidden and mysterious as the Pharaohs were, so tied up with the crops and the people's welfare that if he fails in mind or body he must be got rid of and a successor found. Often he marries a sister-wife as a Pharaoh did; she and his mother are equally important, for they are the representatives of the woman-powers. In some states he goes through rituals which echo those of Egypt and this seems to have gone on in some places almost to the present day. Yet neither kings nor priests are in any sense Egyptian; all that is far back, a memory of something that once happened. Or perhaps, even, we are mistaken to think of Egypt; the pattern and ritual of god-kings may be a pattern which the human mind likes to fall into at one particular stage of its evolution from then to now.

These god-kings were from one point of view lifted out of the ordinary processes of death and decay. They must represent continuity : a going on from past and the ancestors into future and the children's children. We know that in some kingdoms a wooden roof was put over a dead king and he was buried in preparation for his future or continuing life with household goods, slaves and wives. This is of course not exclusively an African idea. In Europe my own northern Saxon and Norse forebears did much the same. It may even be that the servants buried with the dead king felt themselves privileged, partakers of his eternal life. They, as well as the wives, may have hoped to be chosen to follow him, for if they were not chosen they might never have anything beyond ordinary mortality. People perhaps thought of death differently from how most people, at least in America and western Europe, do now; it happened more often, more easily and more publicly. Life was less pleasant, so death less feared. The Egyptians had an immensely complex way of death, of dealing with the various gods and powers from the first serpent to the last pinch of soul dust in the scales of judgment. All this was supervised in detail by the priesthood. This elaborate way could hardly have survived the wanderings and intermarriage of the invaders. But it seems often to have been assumed that at least for the kings some way into another world did exist.

TIME CHART
Ninth Century

Africa. The early west African States are flourishing. They include Ghana, Kanem, Songhai. Mali was still a small state, Darfur was probably in existence. Some of the ruling families were Moslem.

Egypt had been conquered by the Arabs, but Nubia and Ethiopia were separate, mainly Christian kingdoms.

South Europe and the Mediterranean. Steady Arab conquest of south Europe, Spain and all north Africa. Early in the century the Arabs adopted Indian numerals, including zero, which were then generally adopted in Europe. Cotton was imported into Sicily. In Baghdad the Arabs began to take note of the knowledge and philosophy of classical Europe, on which they built a new scientific structure.

The Byzantine Empire still centred on Constantinople, and spreading eastwards.

North Europe. 871-901 Alfred the Great in England. Old centre of power moves north under Charlemagne, but Popes remain in Rome. The early churches built. Invasion by Norsemen and Danes who establish bases in France and England. After Harald Hairfair starts feudalism in Norway, many Norsemen emigrate, some to the recently discovered Iceland. The Sagas of Beowulf and Gudrun take form. Paris becoming an intellectual centre. European reaction against Islam.

India. The temple caves of Ellora built and painted. Buddhism largely accepted.

China. The T'ang dynasty. Unsurpassed beauty of porcelain and other artefacts. High point of Korean and Chinese civilisation. The examination system for the civil service is brought to a fine point. Buddhism spreads, but comes into conflict with the Confucian philosophy. Paper money is printed in China. Many painters and poets.

South-east Asia. The height of Khmer civilisation.

Japan. Many Buddhist buildings and sculptures. Culture follows Chinese examples until (895) the Fujiwara family take over the rule and turn the culture in a nationally different direction.

The states which were made by the invaders probably all date from some time during the first thousand years AD, the time when England was gradually coming into being, welded together by men like Alfred who could only just read and write but who had the feeling for state-craft and the sense that a country is more than the rule of one family. Not all makers of European states felt that. In some it was far more important to know to which baron or duke one owed allegiance than to which king and country, and this went on well into the Middle Ages. The same in Africa.

All states are based on two things: defence and taxation. Taxes may go to defence and one only has to look round now to see how in all the so-called 'civilised' countries this eats up millions and millions of pounds for weapons which, if they were ever used, would destroy the world. Or else taxes go to things which the rulers want. In the democracies, the rulers, if they really represent the people who elect them, want things like housing, education, health services, the arts, and so on, and increasingly in the last century or so, they want things which are demanded by the public conscience. This may, for instance, in some of the industrialised countries, include aid to underdeveloped countries. A great many ordinary voters in the rich states genuinely want to help without thinking whether they will get anything back. A little of this taxation may also go to the international organisations which help people, but not yet enough. Unhappily 'defence' is always a priority.

Apart from the successor states at Meroe, the first entirely African states that we know about are Ghana—well to the north of present-day Ghana—and Kanem. We call these the Sudanic states, not in the sense that they were in any way related to the modern Sudan, but because they lie in the area of grassland and moderate rainfall south of the Sahara and north of the thick forest. They must have been run for a long time—many centuries perhaps—on a basis of tax-gatherers and taxed: pomp and show and heavy consumption by kings and priests in palaces and temples, or, after life is over, in death-defying tombs, and on the other hand villages where crops were grown, cattle, sheep and goats were pastured. To begin with the kings and priests and the tax-gatherers, the counters of wealth and supervisors of trade, were or had been incomers and conquerors, rather different in looks and language and custom from the villagers, though of course equally African. They may have been the men of the iron weapons, for often the king was also (like the Norse god Thor) a smith, a divine forger of swords and thunderbolts. And doubtless he protected his villages against raiding or conquest from other kings or states. So in a good year the taxes might not appear too burdensome, and gradually the two kinds of people intermarried and mingled.

It may be that another important means of conquest had been the horse, carrying the armed horsemen who must have seemed at first as difficult to stand up to as an armoured car or tank does nowadays. The latest series of paintings from the Sahara shows horses and chariots. We know too that useful camels spread west from Egypt along the Mediterranean and then south, leaving their poor bones all along the trade routes that went north and south between one carefully marked water supply and the next.

During the first three centuries AD northern Africa was part of the Roman empire and because the people who lived in it were highly literate and because there are still so many remains of Roman cities, some of which were certainly at the northern end of a great trade route, we know a great deal about their lives. We know that the north African provinces were particularly fertile and that the country which is now desert was then corn- and olive-bearing. Along the south-western Mediterranean there were Latin-speaking Roman colonies which kept up Roman traditions; when Rome became Christian so did they. In the south-east, there were old Greek colonies, many centuries older, like the city of Kyrene in north Africa, whose broad central avenue, with its splendid statues and buildings, was so much admired in the ancient world. And there were newer foundations like Alexander's Egyptian Alexandria, which were mainly Greek-speaking. There were also, of course, Phoenician trading cities, all wealthy and powerful, though Carthage, the strongest of all, the one which had sent out exploring ships which some think actually rounded the Cape of Good Hope, had been destroyed by Rome.

There were also kingdoms more or less within the Roman empire paying tribute. One is less certain about what kind of people lived in them. King Juba of Numidia who married Cleopatra's daughter Selene, was he, for instance, black or white? No historian tells us; it wasn't anything that mattered, especially in the sun-tanned, olive-skinned, Mediterranean world.

But the Moslem explosion of a new, deeply gripping, violently Seventh Century encouraging religion, broke down the remains of the old Roman Christian civilisation which was by then part of the Byzantine

Empire. It swept from east to west of the southern Mediterranean
coast. Perhaps also it was responsible for driving out the non-
Moslem population from Arabia, and perhaps this had something to do with the foundation of the first royal lines in kingdoms
such as Ghana. But of course people who come riding as conquerors don't bring more than a very few wives with them. They
look for women where they go and even if there is formal 'marriage' with one's pure-line sister, there is probably a very thorough
racial mixture on all levels within a couple of centuries. This
always happens in all countries and makes complete nonsense of
proud family pedigrees such, for instance, as my own. Many
present-day African rulers have pedigrees that go back and back
into legend, often beginning with the sudden appearance of a
semi-divine founder with special powers or (like Adam) a 'son
of god'. Sometimes this may be taken as evidence of an incoming,
conquering dynasty, but I don't think we should make too much
of it nor should we suppose that the founders were in some way
non-African, some 'superior' race.

When the Arabs broke out from Arabia their tribalism had
been completely overcome by the inspiration of brotherhood,
which is still the most vital thing about Islam. They set up waves
of fear and retreat in other peoples. For a time the trade routes
with the African states would be broken. But gradually the holy
war of conquest settled down into the ordinary exchanges of
goods that make an elaborate civilisation possible. This settling
down meant that very soon the successful people became rich and
the brother who was a less skilled bargainer and trader was thrust
down into poverty. So the first brotherhood began to break up;
Islam became divided.

It is divided still, and like many religions, it means different
things to different people. Europeans are apt to think of it as they
see it in the Middle East, with veiled and secluded women in
what is very clearly a man's world. But that wouldn't make sense
in some of the coastal states of west Africa where the bulk of the
trading and dealing with money is done by women, most of whom
are at least nominally Moslem. It is the religion that changes,
not the women. On the other hand, in the Hausa area, it is the
men who have the trading skills; the women tend to be left at
home.

By the middle of the seventh century, Egypt had been completely conquered by the Arabs but they were checked in Nubia by the highly skilled bowmen: black African certainly. The final treaty between Egypt and Nubia was a trade agreement. The Arabs sent in food, horses and cloth to Nubia. Nubia sent up slaves to Egypt, 360 a year, not many by later standards but the beginning of something bad.

In a sense no doubt there were slaves everywhere in all continents of the ancient world wherever people fought one another and spared some of the enemy instead of killing them, wherever there was legal punishment, or wherever people got in debt to one another and had nothing to pay with but their bodies. But that is not slave trade. In all the accounts of early trading, between whatever countries, there is usually some mention of slaves. But these slaves were, so to speak, accidental; they were not deliberately hunted. Probably even the Nubians exported to Egypt would have been slaves anyhow.

And south of Nubia? Here we are no longer sure; again we are out of range of written history. We have to count on the archaeologists and the various modern techniques of dating. We can only say that there were probably kingdoms, there was probably trade, though probably again nothing so well organised as the western Sudanic states such as Ghana. It may well be, all the same, that much can yet be discovered, especially when local historians begin to translate their own poems and songs as well as sifting other evidence. For instance, according to A. Kogane, there are 176 great dynastic poems preserved in Ruanda from the eleventh century. They may give some of the names and stories which make history come alive. Islam never got to these far kingdoms. For the Islamic world, as for the Greek world and equally for the English world up till a century ago, the Nile source was fabulous and infinitely far, though it was often imagined as a realm of marvellous riches, perhaps of magic and danger. Yet all this time people were probably living round Lake Victoria, catching fish, growing some kind of grain and gathering fruit and roots wherever they could clear the wild forest away from that splendidly fertile soil where abundant rainfall makes everything possible. It is difficult to imagine the Uganda scene without bananas, without maize or coffee, or many of the modern fruits and vegetables; but perhaps people were healthier before they were stuffed with *matoke*, the boiled bananas which make up only too much of their present-day diet. Surely they sometimes stopped to watch the tremendous thundering, enormously powerful outpouring of the White Nile! They must have wondered where it went.

And again people were certainly living round the upland sources of the Blue Nile. But they had not 'discovered' the mouth of the Nile any more than the Mediterranean people had discovered its ending.

We must also remember that there were still many wanderers in Africa, people who are now called nomadic. Most of them depended on cattle, though some only drank milk, never or seldom actually eating cattle meat; for such people cattle were not only wealth but beauty, the material for song and dance and praise. Some people still move over regular routes with their cattle, like the Fulani who follow regular routes from the northern grazing grounds south to the coastal states of west Africa.

But an existence of this kind means the acquiring of fewer and fewer things in relation to the rest of the world which is, sensibly or not, intent on obeying the advertisers and acquiring more and more things. So the wanderers, Masai, Bushmen, or in Europe gipsies or tinkers, still others in Asia, lose status and are increasingly circumscribed in their wanderings and bullied by the settled people.

And again there were, until quite recently, many cattle-owning people, especially among the Bantu who had more or less permanent settlements, but whose young men herded enormous flocks of cattle or other grazers over wide areas which nobody even dreamed could one day be considered private property and shut against them. This made for fighting situations; the young men were the young warriors. They must also of course be brave against wild beasts, constantly risking their lives against lion or leopard. The women stayed at home, doing the equally useful, but less interesting and less well thought of work of cultivation. This may mean that men get used to doing more adventurous things, which include taking in new ideas, and women tend to do things in the old hard way. Now that there is no more free land in the Republic of South Africa and less and less elsewhere, so that the cattle herding pattern is no longer possible, I ask my girl readers whether there is any reason why this kind of division between adventurous boys and unadventurous girls, should still go on?

Three

Islam and the Sudanic Kingdoms

1066 About the time when William the Conqueror invaded England,
when the Saxon King Harold was killed in the slaughter of Hast-
ings, there was invasion and bloodshed in north Africa. The
Berber tribes were Moslem and there were Berber traders and
governors in the great north African cities, some of which dated
from Roman times, and where there were usually tough little
Christian minorities persecuted or tolerated. But the Bedouin invaders, Arabs from upper Egypt, swept down and broke up much
of the remaining civilisation until they too were caught into the
net of trade and riches and the life of cities.

The Moslem trade network along the Mediterranean coast was
so close-knit that a draft on an eastern Arab bank would be
honoured at a western one. All this was very convenient for the
trade routes where merchants could cross the desert area one way
and come back another. Sicily too, as a largely Arab colony,
joined in the trade prosperity, though not for long, as the
colonists and their businesses were driven out a few generations
later in a Christian re-conquest. But Spain went on for much
longer under Moslem dynasties; science and the arts flourished,
especially architecture. But little of this went south of the
Maghreb.

In this Moslem world one sees the recurring pattern of religious
breakdown, the pure doctrine of Islam corrupted, overlaid by
local custom : accepting local gods or half-gods, accepting habits
and ways of life not sanctioned by the Koran, forgetting that
There is no God but God and Mohammed is his Prophet. Then
comes some event—a pilgrimage to Mecca by a king, the arrival
of some saint or learned man, and the whole thing is revived,

very often bringing with it the will to conversion and conquest. For Islam, which assures the believer of heaven, was a religion which gave that extra strength which people need before the will to war and destruction gets the better of the other and gentler human instincts.

However trade survived. Ghana and Kanem, the great Niger states, went on sending caravans north. But increasingly the south-bound caravans carried conversion with them and also probably Arabic. Good trading demands a common language. Very soon the kings and upper classes of Ghana became Moslems. It was probably a sign of status and friendship with the north, and perhaps was more acceptable to deeper thinking and increasingly civilised societies than the paganism which it superseded and which sometimes included human sacrifice or ritual disfigurement. Yet when the Arab geographer, al-Bakri, described Ghana in 1067, the king still lived in a town called The Forest, six miles from a flourishing Moslem trading city, though the part between the two had been built over, and it sounds as though the king himself, to whom all gold nuggets by right belonged, still practised the ancient rites, though most of his ministers were Moslems.

The Almoravids, Berbers of the north-west coast lands, who became fired with longing for Islamic great deeds, which took some of them on to the conquest of Spain and others to the founding of Marrakesh, later the capital of Morocco, began also to look south, to the far end of the caravan routes. Ghana was the goal—Ghana the fountain of gold. But Ghana held out for many years. In the end the Ghanaian capital was taken and plundered, the conquered were forced to become Moslems and the whole system of central government and taxation broke up. People lapsed back into tribal defence groups. But not for long. Further south along the upper Niger there were Mande people who could and did run an empire of their own, the state of Mali which superseded Ghana. Sundiata, the first Mansa of Mali, hero of a major epic poem, became a Moslem, a legendary master of *djinns*, and following him, the line of rulers for two centuries or more were all believers. They began to establish schools and colleges and so did the other Sudanic Moslem rulers whether independent of Mali or for a time owing allegiance.

The colleges of Timbuktu were famous throughout the Islamic

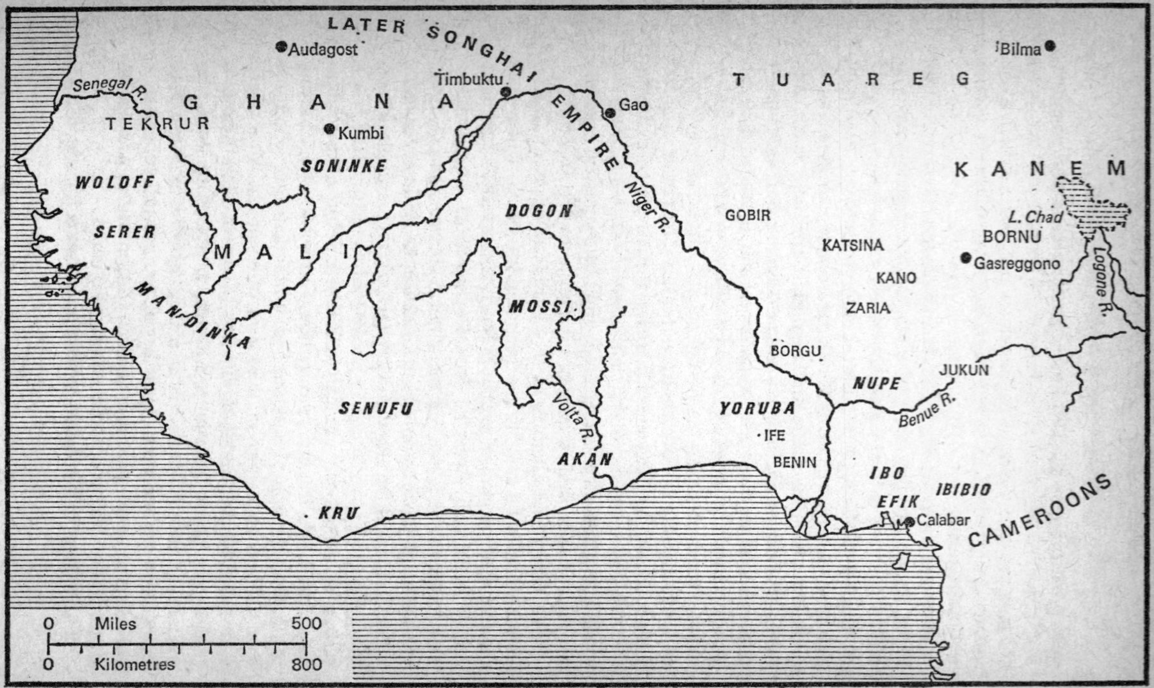
LATER SONGHAI EMPIRE
Audagost
Timbuktu
Gao
Bilma
T U A R E G
K A N E M
Senegal R.
G H A N A
TEKRUR
Kumbi
SONINKE
WOLOFF
SERER
M A L I
MANDINKA
DOGON
Niger R.
MOSSI
GOBIR
KATSINA
KANO
ZARIA
L. Chad
BORNU
Gasreggono
Logone R.
BORGU
JUKUN
NUPE
Benue R.
YORUBA
IFE
BENIN
SENUFU
Volta R.
AKAN
KRU
IBO
IBIBIO
EFIK
Calabar
CAMEROONS
0 Miles 500
0 Kilometres 800

Map 3

world, just as the colleges of Pavia, Paris, Salamanca, Oxford, Cambridge and St. Andrews were famous in the Christian mediaeval world. Scholars and teachers came there to argue and found schools of Islamic theology. Probably, as now in Cairo, most of the teaching was done in the shaded arcades of the mosques. As today, students from Ghana and Mali went to other universities where they often had national hostels; they may well have studied mathematics, astronomy and geography as well as theology, but no doubt the ban on representational art was as strongly enforced then as now, and probably the ban on alcohol. All literacy was, of course, in Arabic; a rather later writer says 'There is a big demand for books in manuscript . . . more profit is made from the book trade than from any other line of business.' Probably no one thought of writing the native speech of Mali or Songhai; that was only for talking or songs, though some were good enough to hand down from one generation to the next, just as the Homeric poems were handed down and as the long Sundiata epic has been. We are lucky that such invaluable material has now been written down, as the wrath of Sundiata has been, by the Mali historian, Niane. If this is not done now, people who have begun to read newspapers, comics, political pamphlets and such ephemera, might cease to be interested in their own splendid oral history; those that know it might then become discouraged and die without passing it on. It is, however, most peculiar that there are no state records of the kind which one might expect, either in Arabic or in any other language. These large states could not possibly have run their taxation systems let alone anything else, without keeping records and lists, even if there were trained, professional 'rememberers'. What happened to their records? Were they on some type of flimsy material which has just disappeared? Were they eaten by termites, destroyed by mould or burnt by conquerors? One would have expected that enough would have survived somewhere to give us a clue. Perhaps something will turn up, if not within the borders of the ancient empires then somewhere else, for the people of these states were travellers. One of the Mali emperors, the Mansa Musa, made the pilgrimage to Mecca, astonishing Egypt with his lavish distribution of gold and bringing back an architect from Arabic Spain to build mosques and palaces.

Thirteenth Century

Africa. In the west Mali is the dominant empire, Sundiata, the Keita emperor, having conquered the Susu and dominated Ghana in the middle of the century. Songhai is part of the Mali sphere of influence. Bornu and Kanem are both trading states. Strong Moslem trading and religious influence. Hausa kingdoms beginning to form. Possible beginnings of Akan states.

The kingdom of Dongola, in the area which was Nubia, is still Christian. So is Ethiopia, but Arabs control the sea ports. Darfur is an important Moslem trading state.

The Almoravid Empire has spread and been succeeded by the Almohads, but now the Maghreb is divided into three kingdoms, which in turn, were to fall to various victors.

Probably about now the Kingdom of Kongo under Ntinu Wene, begins to take form. Possibly other kingdoms in central Africa, of which little trace remains.

Mediterranean. Various crusades undertaken. 1202-1204 fourth crusade ends in taking of Constantinople by crusaders and end of Byzantine empire. Beginning of Turkish takeover. 1220 Crusade against Egypt fails. 1270 Seventh and last crusade. 1250 Mamelukes, in Egypt.

Europe. Constant struggle between Empire and Papacy involving all European countries at one time or another. Kings occasionally excommunicated. But present national boundaries forming. Beginning of the rise of the cities and trading power. The Hansa towns start.

In spite of this the main cathedrals are finished, built or begun : Laon, Reims, Chartres, Tournai, Sainte Chapelle; Westminster Abbey, Peterborough; Coimbra, Burgos; Bamberg, Sienna. Also Town Halls especially in Germany. Universities founded, including Padua, Toulouse, University College Oxford and then Balliol, Peterhouse Cambridge, and Lisbon; National Colleges built at Paris.

The Franciscan order established and working. 1215 Magna Carta sealed by King John. 1265 Simon de Montfort summons the first English Parliament with representatives of shires, cities and boroughs. Cimabue painting. Among authors : Snorri Stur-

Iason, author of *Heimskringla Saga,* Roger Bacon, Saxo Grammaticus of Denmark, Dante writing at end of century. Among books and poems: *The Harrowing of Hell, Huon of Bordeaux, Roman de la Rose, Carmina Burana, Thidreks Saga, 'Sumer is icumen in'.* First Sonnets. Minnesingers and wandering singer-politicians as Walter von der Vogelweide. Troubadours. Folk music. The Albigensian heresy ruthlessly suppressed. 1273 Thomas Aquinas publishes *Summa Theologica.* Beginnings of genuine national feeling in Holland. Scotland in revolt against English overlords.

Further east. 1211 to 1277 Genghis Khan invades China, north India, Samarkand, Persia, Russia with vast slaughter.

1238 Mongols take Moscow and establish the Golden Horde. 1241 They sack Budapest and Breslau.

Persian faience at its height. Saadi writes *The Diwan* and *The Rose Garden.* 1271-1295 Marco Polo travels through Asia and is for some years in the service of Kublai Khan in China.

India. Brahmin power in most kingdoms, with suppression of Buddhism. Temple of Konerak and others.

China. Sung period, followed by Yuan. High civilisation with distaste for outside influence. Painters, poets.

Japan. Internal development. Shinto cult. Rolls of pictures, including lively satire.

America. Beginnings of the Inca states around Cuzco in the Andes. Massive building. Sun worship. Chimu culture in Peru. Use of potato.

But the empire of Songhai succeeded that of Mali, though perhaps the ordinary village people didn't much care who ruled them so long as it was not an oppressive rule. They were used to paying taxes. Probably they were not much interested in Islam, regarding it as something for rulers and merchants. These were sizable states stretching a third of the way or more across Africa. But they were on the whole in the fairly open country of the savannahs, between the desert and the heavy rain-wet forest near the southern coast, part of which was later to be known as Guinea.

What was happening there? Well, this was a highly productive region. Here was gold, ivory from the forest elephants, beautiful leopard and monkey skins, cola nuts which luckily the Prophet had not known about or he might have forbidden them, but perhaps not yet palm wine. But there could not have been close-set farm gardens such as one sees today, before the South American food-plants were brought in, nor could there have been anything like the same population. What is clear is that the forest people lived in big villages and certainly had enough leisure and prosperity to make beautiful things, carvings and pottery and ornaments of gold for people or shrines. They knew how to make representations of people, animals and plants, either in splendid naturalism such as we see in the Ife bronzes, which are only a little later on in time, or in the stylized forms which shocked Victorian missionaries and administrators but are now so much admired. It is curious that Islam, which forbade the representation of human or animal forms and drove the artists of north Africa into an almost barren stylisation, appears to have had little effect on the west African converts.

That is to say there was a forest culture or civilisation along the 'Guinea coast'; there were holy places or shrines around them; ordered groupings of houses on the courtyard principle of several single storey, lightly built houses, round or square, inside one wall, the outer shell, so to speak, of a complex family relationship in which obligations and duties were well known. It is frightening to live in forest country; beyond the village clearing the ghosts begin. Perhaps it has something to do with the illnesses and infections which flourish in this kind of climate unless and until modern preventive medicine comes in. Some of them are quick killers, others slowly nibble away at health and strength. Some are hideously disfiguring or painful, looking as though they must be the deliberate work of man-hating forces. There are poisonous plants. Wild beasts leap out of the dark, claw and kill. There are noises that you cannot name and clear up.

Probably people had musical instruments early on, especially percussion. The history of drums goes far back and the drum rhythm and drum talk was to develop over centuries, taking the place of writing as a means of communication. Songs, like poetry or sculpture, become stylized; words take on layers of meanings and are used to transfer these meanings to things, which then, in a sense, come alive. Science perhaps has less chance in the forest, where it is hard to see the stars which develop the beginnings of astronomy, the first step in our endless curiosity away from the problems of self and out towards the poles and the constellations.

There would certainly have been regular markets and known tracks through the forest. Probably the early trade was with small kings and chiefs. The Akan states were the first we know about, and then, further east, Ife the birth place of gods—a centre and dispersal point as Delphi was for the Hellenic world. Here were the beginnings of the Yoruba nations and of Benin. It is the spiritual centre for the Yoruba but the Oni of Ife also had some political authority even when Oyo was the most powerful of the Yoruba states.

Dating is difficult again. If there were better records it would all be much easier. But the culture and continuity of these states, as of others in Africa, was to be broken by the slave trade. If you lived on the assumption that the rememberers, the keepers of oral history, and the authorities on what to say, dance, do, think and make, would in due time pass on their knowledge to their duly chosen successors, and then suddenly, the old men, useless as slaves, were killed, and the young ones, perhaps with the history half learnt, carried off to the plantations, you have a break like that of the European Dark Ages. What we do know is that, before the slave trade got going, when the Portuguese came in the fifteenth century they found states which had been going on for a long time, ceremonials and rituals dating back beyond the memory of the fathers' fathers.

Islam never seems to have touched the real forest people, the dwellers in darkness. But thousands of miles away on the east coast of Africa it had spread down from one trading post to the next, starting on the Red Sea. Each port would have some kind of small state behind it, guarding and feeding it; there would be reasonably fixed custom dues; and whatever else it had not got it would certainly have a mosque and baths. There would be a nucleus of Arab traders.

But were they the first? It is fairly certain that there had been overseas trading with the African interior long before Islam, first through Egypt, then increasingly with the Mediterranean world in the early centuries AD. Coins fortunately survive in difficult climatic conditions; the coins that have been found on the east coast are mostly Roman though the trading ships which brought them may easily have been Greek. The first written account is the Periplus of the Erythrean Sea, dating from the first or second century. This shows the imports from the Meditterranean world, of dyed cloth (probably purple-dyed), silver, copper and tin, wine and drinking cups; luxury goods on the whole, which must have made a good profit. The return cargoes would consist of spices, incense, tortoiseshell and ivory, equally luxurious and profitable.

There was certainly also trade with India, dating back at least two thousand years. This is something one would expect, given the highly organised state of the south Indian kingdoms, still more the Sumatra maritime kingdom. It seems as though the original settlers in Madagascar may have come from there. India sent cotton, cloth and foodstuffs, including sugar. And of course once one gets to Sumatra it is not far to China, an old civilisation by that time, but not uninterested in the barbarian world whether black or white. Their main export would probably be porcelain and there are still barrow-loads of broken Chinese jars and plates to be found in east African palaces, burial and trading sites, often now lost in the tangles of thick forest. This again would probably have meant trading posts and people wanting their own kind of culture and cookery. And this in turn might have meant the introduction of Asian plants, including two very important ones— bananas and coconuts. Much of Tanzania looks like south India over again, across the unimpeding sea.

Perhaps it was the introduction of these two quick and easily-grown crops which brought the Bantu population north along the coast some five centuries ago (see Chapter 8). This was another of those slow movements of peoples wandering and settling and then wandering again. These were Negro peoples, short-nosed with really black skins and very short springs of hair; in time their northern wanderings would bring them into contact with the lighter-skinned narrow-nosed Somali people, speaking a different language, with different manners and customs.

It is important to remember that there were constant invasions and movements of people from the earliest times until almost now. Many came from the upper Nile and often, after they had found a fertile place and settled with or without the consent of other peoples, they would remain more or less separate, keeping up their own special customs or ways of life, though sometimes they would join up with others. This resulted, for one thing, in the network of tribes and language groups in what is now Kenya, Uganda and Tanzania and in some parts of which there are still 'submerged classes', not slaves, but looked down upon and with different manners, customs and skills.

Trade does not seem to have gone far inland, not certainly as far as the Great Lakes. But there were routes to the main producing districts of Zimbabwe and perhaps the copper mines of Katanga. References in near contemporary documents are few and far between. But remains of Indian beads and Chinese porcelain were found at the great Zimbabwe (see Chapter 8).

The gap between the early trade of which Roman coins supply the evidence and the later Arab trade came because of the bursting out of Islam which cut most of the ordinary contact between the Mediterranean and the Christian Axum or Abyssinia. Yet this upland state went on keeping up its own vision of Christianity, which gradually became more remote from that of Europe. The Abyssinians had to defend themselves against the pagans to the south and develop into a great fighting country which later on was to attack the small Moslem trading states along the coast (see Chapter 8).

Four

The African Moral Order

So far this history of Africa looks like invasions, war, rulers and ruled. And that is what a calendar of historical events is likely to be. History only happens when there is change. Most people don't like change. They try to avoid it even if in the end it may be better for them. What happens when there is nothing we call history, when change is so slow that from year to year nobody notices it?

One thing is that language develops. But not all languages develop alike or are useful for the same thing. Some languages develop in the direction of accuracy, and most European languages are of this kind. They break up words and ideas and partly analyse them so that you can see what they are made of. Words in ordinary use get shorter and simpler instead of longer. In English for instance we talk of an old red cow with straight horns or a young black cow which has been badly fed. You see at once which things are of the same kind in each phrase. But in some African languages there may be a single word for each kind of cow in which it can be quite hard to find the separate stems. For example there are the Setswana descriptive words : separate stems, prefixed by *kgomo,* the word for any kind of cattle beast : *kgomo e makoro* (with horns pointing inward), *kgomo e kwebana* (plain red head, body red spotted on white but with streaks of plain red on back and belly), *kgomo e tshumuphefaadu* (ox with white forehead and black and white on body), or *kgomo e kgwanaphefaadu* (background red with white starry or triangular spots, but with a white wavy line on the side).

Yet these may be in themselves expressive and interesting

words. Setswana for instance strikes me as essentially good for poetry, singing and some kinds of conversation. It is not a limited language; it could probably express anything but in an unanalytic, perhaps roundabout and very lengthy way. Chinese, where whole concepts are gathered up into a single written character, and where learning the characters is an education in itself, and takes years, is also bad for science. So nowadays Chinese is being altered accordingly. Perhaps African languages will be modified in the same way or perhaps they will be kept for, speech, poetry, fiction and drama, while English or French is used as a useful written language of non-poetic communication. This is roughly what has happened in India and seems to be a practical solution.

The other thing I notice about Setswana is a piling-on of verbal allusions, especially in songs, in an almost riddling way. One thing recalls another in the mind and tone of the singer or speaker of praises. One can tell a good deal about people by the way their speech is made up; language and its speakers influence one another. In Gaelic, for instance, the old language of the Scottish Highlands, there is no possessive. All is done with adverbs : love is at me on you. This may well be a more accurate way of describing some kinds of relationships than the direct possessive grab of English.

Probably the Bantu languages and, I believe, many of the west coast languages are specially good for remembering some kinds of things with great vividness and delicacy and expressing certain kinds of social and personal relations. These languages were not written down until after the missions came. It is a fact that if people learn to use a written language—especially if they get so much into the grip of it that they are genuinely unhappy without something to occupy their reading, roving eyes—they will be less good at speech. They will tend to cut it down as people do in European or American towns, clipping and shortening, using quick easy slang. And then memories for long episodes will weaken; descriptions and conversations will be cut out; the material of good narrative will be lost. It may well be that in the process of acquiring literacy much African history has been and still will be forgotten. It is quite clear that this has happened already in many parts of Africa. One hopes that there are now enough Africans aware of this danger to find and collect what is left while there is still time.

The first impact of 'civilisation' and the new language that went with it, was to cut Africans off from their own past, making some of them feel that it was worthless, others that it was unprogressive, something to be ashamed of. But it is very dangerous for people to be cut off from their past and their ancestors, which is also the basic material of their self respect and their moral certainty. If there is something equally strong to put in place of the past it may be possible. Christianity was sometimes that; so may Communism be. But do either of them last for long enough in the African tide of life as abiding moral certainties to make up for the long past?

No people exist without some kind of moral and social framework and when this is not written down it may be strongest, as the unwritten-down British constitution seems to be. A social framework is normally a set of checks and balances to keep things from altering too quickly, but allowing them to alter enough to meet new needs as they arise. Sometimes the need to change becomes very urgent, as when new technologies arise, and then the social framework gets badly strained unless people are brave and intelligent enough to alter it deliberately. A moral framework of philosophy has to try and make people happy in the sense of allowing or helping them to be what they want to be. To do this it creates myths—stories of great poetic strength and value—and the gods that go appropriately with these myths. In all societies there are what anthropologists call rites of passage from unborn-ness to birth, from childhood to man- or womanhood, from life to death. These are the difficult moments for which we make our myths.

All over Africa there has been some kind of philosophy of life and a moral order, which was sometimes made plain in a hierarchy of gods or half-gods, spirits or powers, and which comprehended past and future, and all life. The forms it takes or took are, of course, very varied, some being apparently illogical or arbitrary, but there does appear to be a basic pattern. The past, as in many moral orders, including that of Confucius, was represented by the ancestors, the future by the young initiates. All African societies have practised some kind of initiation, that is, the rite of passage between childhood and maturity. The moral order is based on the survival, not of the individual but of the group, the family or the tribe.

The African moral order was not on the whole thought of in terms of individual self salvation. This is a Mediterranean idea which has gradually spread and is, of course, basic to Christianity as it was to the rather earlier mystery religions. When it is allied to the idea of individual success, that is to say competition, it is very disruptive of a society which is based less selfishly on larger groups. Europeans and European-educated Africans feel that a moral order based on a nation has a certain respectability, that the American or British, French or German ethos is something for which men and women must give their lives, though this idea has been broken into by what happens in modern warfare. But it is felt that a smaller group is not only a nuisance in a highly organised society, but produces wrong loyalties. This attitude has been reflected in modern African politics, especially in anti-tribalism by the modern politicians. Yet the politicians have often been strong and loyal trade unionists. Why should a trade union be considered morally better than a tribe? Because it is 'modern'? Because it is on a European pattern? Because it is only economic —but is it? In fact the wisest African politicians defend the morality of the tribe and see how it must become part of their national future.

Kenneth Kaunda in *A Humanist in Africa* gives his version of what he calls the African philosophy of man and I call the African moral order. We speak of the same things and he writes of the impact 'of centuries of existence within tribal society', showing how it was a mutual society and an accepting community which did not take account of failure, but valued people 'not for what they could achieve, but because they were *there*'. He then writes of the tribe being an inclusive society with its wide spread of mutual responsibility. President Kaunda is building Zambia, but this is the base on which he builds. Tom Mboya, one of the builders of Kenya, wrote very sensibly of positive and negative tribalism. And of course the picture of tribal organisation in Jomo Kenyatta's *Facing Mount Kenya* is still highly relevant. Note, for instance 'the land not only unites the living members of the tribe, but also the dead ancestors and the unborn posterity'.

Other leaders in various parts of Africa have, equally, understood that the tribes are the building blocks of the country. Probably each has his own tribal environment partly in mind—why not? I too remember that I am both a Scot and a Mokgatla; two loyalties keep me on my toes and make me, I believe, more interested in the United Nations and more convinced of the necessity for practical and universal human brotherhood than I would be if I had less close loyalties.

When there was no alternative, the African moral order or philosophy of man expressed through tribe or nation was kept in balance by magic, sacrifice, smelling out of witches and so on. This gave solidarity but was often demonstrably cruel and unjust to the individual. But if you thought this was the only way to avert more general disaster it had to happen, as in the days of the Republic of Rome when a terrifying earthquake crack opened in the Roman forum and Curtius leapt into it as a voluntary sacrifice to the angry gods. With the coming of science there are better ways of averting disaster.

The African view of the moral order means a different view of justice or of the functioning of any Court of law. Europeans with their sharp vision of heaven and hell, demand that there must be clear innocence or guilt. But if the idea is to restore the moral order you have to go deeper, allowing for motive, customs, relationships and all the rest that make up the full human situation. If this were fully worked out it would be perfect, but it would take a very long time. As it is, an African 'trial' in *kgotla*, or whatever corresponds to that, does take a long time and nobody hurries it, for it involves more than just a man's life, it is a disturbance of everything. But it is often far from perfect, because it may in practice allow all sorts of wrong motives, favouritism, bribery beforehand of those who are supposed to know custom or precedent, and so on, to creep in. This happens more easily when there is no written law. An innocent but unattractive person will not get off so easily in *kgotla* as in a Magistrate's Court, though here too there may be illogical prejudice. Yet supposing a man has committed something which is formally a crime, but may have done it for some intelligible and perhaps 'good' reason, given the context of the society he lives in and accepts, such as inducing rain to fall on parched tribal land, he may have more chance of being understood in *kgotla* and not being punished as a criminal.

The principle of compensation to an injured person is basic to African law, at any rate in most parts of Africa, and probably has been so for a long time. It was clearly recognised in Northern Europe by Saxon and Germanic law but tended to disappear in feudal times when brawling became a breach of 'the King's peace' and the individual was only the smallest unit of the feudal pattern. Compensation is now being brought back into English criminal law, but the young tough does not actually pay it himself to the old woman he has coshed; in fact he is not made either to feel morally guilty or to try to purge his guilt by the direct confrontation that would happen under most African law. In Africa compensation is no doubt open to bargaining and if a man is fined so many head of cattle he may get away with giving half the number to the person he has injured. Probably the injured person asks for more than he or she thinks they will get and the court or the elders or the chief, who is still the final authority, will probably not suppose that the man who has committed the injury will pay all he has been asked to pay. But if he is caught a second time on the same offence, he may be made to pay the whole of the original fine, so it is definitely a deterrent.

In southern Africa at least, public beating tends to be a punishment for unsocial behaviour, or if a young man is fined and his father thinks he does not deserve to have the cattle found for him, he may be beaten instead. This may well be now becoming more unacceptable. However, if you take your own law and custom seriously you will pay less attention to that of other people. Imprisonment by a white man's court for a crime which may not even be considered as serious carries no stigma. In fact you may be thought rather clever to have got out of your difficulties with, say, a fortnight in prison at the government's expense, and no fine of oxen or even goats demanded. On the other hand, a long prison sentence is thought to be a much more cruel and shocking thing than a severe beating.

There is no space here to go deeply into African concepts of law which, naturally, vary very much in detail in different parts of the huge continent and which have not always been correctly understood or interpreted. I have merely tried to give some account of generally accepted ideas which are genuinely African. In the countries of north and west Africa which have been under Moslem rulers, strict Islamic law has been applied for centuries. Similarly, there has been Christian influence, though not for so long, in countries where Christian missions have been strong. Of course today's independent states have taken over the laws of colonial rulers, especially British and French, wholesale in the upper courts. African lawyers, expensively trained in the European law schools, naturally wish this to continue, even if the law is sometimes inappropriate and often (as indeed in Europe) incomprehensible to the ordinary man. But there is often a dual system with the easily understood 'native law and custom' applying in the lower courts.

However, to go back to the African ideas, another difficulty over the interpretation of crime and punishment is that there is no clear distinction between civil and criminal law in African customary law; this sometimes worries professional lawyers from other cultures. In an African court all punishments are likely to be thought of as being ways of converting an injury to the human community into healing and order. This again goes back to the general African philosophy of a central living force whose highest expression is mankind.

This is in many ways a splendid concept but it has never developed completely. Its intellectual and moral implications have not been thought out but have become lost in a tangle of fears and prohibitions and enforcements, often of a debasing kind, which people accepted because they had become part of a myth, a great story which encouraged and justified their way of living.

Part of the reason why it has never been developed into a real philosophy is because this would have meant a new kind of thinking not in accordance with accepted ways of expression, and this would be impossible because of the respect paid everywhere in Africa to old age, to the person who is thought of as near to the ancestors and the past. Rudeness to an older person brings quick punishment all over the continent. Of course, when an aged man or woman has genuinely collected wisdom out of long experience, it is right and proper that he or she should be listened to. Perhaps this it not done enough in Western societies where so much emphasis is on youth. But it also means that too much belief and attention may be paid to age and precedent and custom. The younger groups are discouraged from questioning. Naturally when they do begin to question—and this happens as soon as they get in touch with new sources of knowledge and technical or commercial ability—they want to break the whole thing up. They must be careful not to break more than they intend. Moral frameworks should not be broken but adapted; it can be done.

However, the main thing to bear in mind about the African moral order is the deflection of interest from the individual to the group. This means a certain conservatism, a tendency to go on doing something that works in the old way even if somebody has thought of a new way of doing it better. It need not do this; in societies which have thought this out more logically, technological advances are welcomed so long as they are for the whole group, not an exploiting individual. But few people in Africa have seen this far. The old way also means disapproval of individual assertion, just as it means courage and endurance in the bearing of individual disasters. Children are brought up together, always with others younger or older than themselves, thus avoiding the individual and sometimes oppressive love and attention of the parents such as is the normal pattern in most developed countries. Instead, all adults act as parents or grandparents; a crying baby expects the nearest woman to pick him up and comfort him. All this tends to produce a society which can go on year after year without developing the stresses which make for power, war, glory, religious conviction or great art. That is to say without the materials of 'history', the memorable phrase, the memorable event. Because of the African moral order always reasserting itself, many parts of Africa remained for many centuries without history.

The group in Africa as elsewhere must have started in the beginning with the family. It grew to become a clan or tribe. The head of it, the chief or whatever corresponded to him (sometimes her) was never thought of as a completely autocratic figure, unless he was a war leader in time of war. He was instead thought of as somebody with a great many responsibilities towards the tribe and between the tribe and other powers, real or imagined, and constantly kept in check by a council, usually of elders. And this is how most of Africa, especially the southern half, was grouped up till fairly lately and sometimes to this day. Yet, this constantly self-stabilising society was not at all simple except to the often unseeing eye of the outsider, especially the outsiders who wanted to change it and supposed the simple savage could easily be made to accept something else. They got it wrong.

There are no loose ends in tribal society. Everyone is held in a network of relationships and these include the dead as well as the living. It makes for closeness, for social classes staying as they are, for carefully exclusive systems of aid and occupation. It also means that there is a welfare society on a poverty level, a level of subsistence, of having enough to eat, but not much more. The orphan and the aged will have some place in it. The sick will not be entirely neglected. Everybody may be undernourished, but few will starve. It was a pre-mission tenet—that the man with two blankets lent one to the man with none. Yet this closed form of social order tends to be very hard on the original-minded man or woman and stops new ideas from taking shape and new techniques from being used.

Tribal society can also be hard on anyone who happens to come in from outside, especially if they get into trouble, as they may easily do unintentionally. They may not be able to catch the exact phrase or action, or become related : is this not known in Western society? Some modern tribal leaders have seen this and tried to break it down, often with the genuine Christian wish for universal brotherhood, or through irritation at the conservatism of some of their friends and relations. And again, tribal feelings may be deliberately used to inflame jealousy, hatred or war which may have had altogether other reasons for starting, to do with power and economics. That is only to say that all human attempts to make a good society have elements in them which can be perverted. All the more reason to try and strengthen the good which is in them as well.

Yet if there is enlightened leadership tribal society need not be against new ideas and techniques, but must be constantly adjusting them and itself. So any leader who plans to keep this kind of society and yet to allow or encourage change has to act very carefully. If he is wise, above all if he is initiated, so that he is not only one of a nation, but also one of a tribe, so that he knows with complete certainty who he is and why he is a man, he will see that there must be continuity between past and future and also between all the people of a tribe, rich and poor, young and old, and that this in turn must lead on to the same continuity elsewhere. This is part of being African, but it might in time bring needed healing to Europe, America and Asia.

That kind of leader will know that the young green branch must grow from the old tree. He cannot afford to throw anything away until he sees the next step. There is so much wisdom in the old traditions that most of them can be adapted. We must never forget that tribal society and the moral order on which it is based has two things which lift it above all but the very best in Europe. For it does not admit the evil of individual competttition and exploitation, and also it makes ordinary people feel safe, safer and less lonely than they are in most modern European societies. When those who have been hurt by it—the original-minded—decide it must go, they have to find something to put in its place which will make people feel equally secure and in a state of moral order and comfort. So far they have not found it.

"Remember you knowledge is limited."

Five

Down the Centuries in West Africa

The clearest line from pre-history to documented history is on the west coast of Africa where one can trace the rise and fall of the smaller kingdoms south of the great Sudanic states. Europe was rather like this after the break-up of the Roman Empire, and might have gone on in the same way for much longer, but that inventions were made and adopted at once which began to put things on to a large scale. Most of these were war inventions, though some like the mill (a Roman invention), the spinning wheel and the horizontal loom, made women's work quicker and easier, and therefore potentially money-making. Yet in some ways the most devastatingly important invention both for intellectual progress and for the dissemination of hatred between peoples with different ideas was the printing press. The inventions which had to do with war tended to make those who adopted them more secure, so that their frontiers would be pushed out. It does not look as though this kind of thing happened much in Africa or only on a smaller, slower scale. The fact that it did not happen made the African states highly vulnerable later on. Yet they continued to improve certain techniques, for instance metal casting. Why one and not the other?

When we come to look at what is known both of the Windward Coast peoples who were little affected by the inland empires of Mali and Songhai, and of the Akan kingdoms, there seems to be little difference in kind between one century and the next, and that was during the period when, in Europe, firearms and printing were both invented. Is this lack of invention what one may expect from a moral order which is always tending to discipline itself, to go back into its old shape, where the strong feeling against change which is normal to most human beings is enforced by custom?

We cannot unfortunately be certain that the accepted chronologies and genealogies of the Akan states, represent the true facts or dates. It is probable that the inland states were founded by incomers, traders in gold or kola nuts, where trading roads or rivers met. There was a state calendar of Bono, but how much reliance can we place on it? If its time corresponds with ours, we may say that the state of Bono lasted from 1295 (but probably in fact later) to 1740 when the last king, Nana Ameyaa Kwaakje, killed himself rather than survive conquest by the Ashanti. The ruins of their capital city, Bono Mansa, are 100 miles north of Kumasi, the Ashanti capital. It must have been always a trading centre to which the northern caravans came, with a big Arab quarter.

It was a city built upon gold, obsessed with gold. The dark bodies of their kings were splendidly dusted with gold, handfuls of gold dust in golden basins. A king wore gold, ate from gold, and this gold, which was perhaps also the sun in men's minds, had power of life and increase over the king's soul, which was also the defence and glory and necessity of the people. If it was taken from them they would shrivel away. Silver was the lifegiver for the queen's soul, and the queens, the sisters and mothers, were as necessary as the kings to the well-being of the state.

Here again, there is a question of records. There were people who, their descendants say, offered prizes for songs and poems. But none of them were written down. This is almost certainly because words and dance and the complex rhythms of married speech and body movements, could not be expressed either in writing or musical notation. It would have been stupid to try. Or was writing considered a less honourable thing than memory, perhaps because everyone can see and touch it, whereas memory is within, untouchable? Or is it something in the actual saying of a word which gives it potency? Akan history, with much other African history, was left under the guard of special rememberers, voices between the past and the future, between the powers and wisdom of the dead, and the actions of the living. Of course we cannot be sure that this was how people thought, only that it is a possible explanation. If it was unthinkable that the stored memory should *not* be passed on (perhaps from father to son or nephew) and then, suddenly, the persons of all the rememberers were destroyed by a more brutal and efficient kind of war, history itself would be destroyed.

Certainly the Arab community of Bono Mansa was able to read and write. One of the queen mothers, Aferanowas, was married twice, to Moslem learned men, perhaps from the Hausa states beyond the river Niger, but she did not introduce records. No doubt her brother or son was by then on the throne, the sacred and elaborate stool which was the symbol of power and godhead. No Moslem was allowed to rule Bono, and perhaps that is another clue to the absence of writing; it may have been thought of as essentially alien, an appurtenance of Allah, but not of their own gods.

However, there are later Arabic manuscripts, though none earlier than the eighteenth century, and all following the conversion of the kings to Islam. A very few of these are in west African languages, though there is a poem with alternate lines in Arabic and Wolof. Most are genealogies, lists of wars and famines or religious material, as well as a handy collection of charms and magic formulae for almost anything, often incorporating a grid of magical numbers. For abstracted numbers appear to be powerful and therefore magic, whereas seven cows are only seven cows. If these manuscripts were being written two hundred years ago, others may have been written three hundred years before that, and it is always excitingly possible that one may turn up.

These Akan kingdoms always reckoned descent through the mother. Like the golden sun, the golden king had no father, or none that counted. And he knew that his direct heir was his sister's son. This is still the social pattern over most of the west coast of Africa, as in parts of south India and many other places. It tends to mean that the child may love his father, who pets him and is more on his own level, but fears and reveres his uncle, his mother's brother, head of the house. Yet it may also be that, if the father is not there, or is with other wives, the child may suffer from feeling fatherless. However, it is certainly a pattern of society which gives women more sexual freedom, at least her husband is not also her lord and master. Possibly this represents the remains of a period of genuine matriarchy (rule by the mothers) which may have been usual over much of Africa—and, indeed, other countries. There are echoes of it in stories of the gods in many places, and also, for example, in Kikuyu legend.

Apart from Bono there were many smaller states, mostly in the bend of the Black Volta, between it and the Niger, in forest and open savannah country. And there were several small states along the coast which, in time, were the first to see the Portuguese ships and begin to trade that way with the outer world, so that gradually sea trade became more important than the northern caravans. There was intermarriage with the Europeans and some of these descendants are still great families in Sierra Leone and elsewhere on the west coast; the Portuguese admired and bought their ivory carvings. The men of the Kru coast were renowned seamen.

These states probably all started as conquering clans or tribes, or broken off bits of tribes, which ended by settling, building towns and trading. There was a group of Mossi states north of the Akan states, but south of Songhai, whose borders were often harassed by the Mossi horsemen. According to the records, some were led by princesses. All took with them a load of sacred objects, above all the chief's stool, without which there could be no chief. The inland tradition always shows a chief and a queen mother. The Denkyra were a powerful forest state in the seventeenth century. But the greatest of all was the Ashanti confederacy.

The Ashanti genealogies go back several centuries, but it was not until the overthrow first of Denkyra, then of Bono, that they became rich and powerful, formally a confederacy, but a very stable one, in time ruling almost down to the coast. Here in the late seventeenth century was a highly organised military and trading state, reasonably well aware of what was going on beyond it. The tactics of Ashanti warfare were elaborate and successful, and as soon as they could buy firearms, probably from the Dutch fort at Elmina, they learnt to use them efficiently. In fact they were probably well able to take advantage of technological advance and to make some, at least, of the social changes which these made necessary, although keeping their main social structure. The Ashanti confederacy was perhaps the most nearly feudal of any African states whose structure is known, though there were elements of an elective situation. In practice, much of the government was decentralised, and controlled by the lesser chiefs, but all could be called up to Kumasi. The records are mostly of war, as all records have been until lately, but clearly this only took place on the basis of material prosperity, largely based on export of gold and a good deal of national enthusiasm. There was also much artistic ability and a high standard of crafts.

Early
eighteenth
century
The great Ashanti prophet, Okomfo Onokye, acting in concert with the ruling statesman, Osei Tutu, made the golden stool of the Asantehene (corresponding to the High King in Celtic countries) as the shrine for the soul of the Ashanti nation, not in a merely formal sense but so that everyone believed and felt that it mattered desperately. It was left to the English to desecrate the stool, unintentionally no doubt, and meaning everything for the best as usual, but destroying something in people's souls which could not be replaced. When Lady Baden-Powell, widow of General Baden-Powell, came to Ghana for the independence celebrations, she brought some of the most valued and valuable bronze coffers, once taken by her husband in war, back to Kumasi. But such things almost always happen too late.

All these west African nations had a definite religion, usually including a rather remote creator god, beyond day-to-day worship or sacrifice, infinitely praiseworthy yet far from the troubles of men. Much more important for ordinary life was, and is, the network of shrines to various lesser gods or spirit powers, some with healing or cursing properties, but liable to be despised and forgotten if they do not produce what is asked for. Respect was always paid to the ancestors, usually with a small libation of some kind of alcohol. All this can be, and often is, in existence, side by side with various kinds of Christianity, believed in, but on a different level and while wearing different clothes.

At certain times the chiefs or kings who now represent some of the west coast clans or states, wear their traditional dress, as I saw them at the time of Ghana independence. Circlets of pure gold weighed on dark brows and arms, splendidly moulded lumps of solid gold swung from knees or sandals. Either they wore little but skins and beads and feathers in a hieratic and splendid nakedness, or the beautiful folds of the many-coloured *kente* cloth hung from their shoulders. Drums boasted their history to those who could interpret them. Had this been in an older day no doubt the spears which were still carried by those who bore the title of executioners of the court, would have drunk blood as proof of power and difference from the ordinary world. As it was the chiefs probably changed back into smart Western suits and the chairmanship of the local co-operative.

What was it like for them to be stared at? Perhaps, before becoming either of the kinds of person whom both they and the onlookers felt they were, they had used words, or had words used on them, in the sense of designating them. This would have helped them to become different. What is designating? Well, the people of Great Britain have seen their own Queen with two separate personalities, marked off by designating words: the Queen crowned in Westminster Abbey with words used partly by those officiating and partly by those, including myself, who shouted formally from the galleries: and the Queen as secular wife and mum, designated by the press and by millions of people everywhere. But in Africa the principle of designation, whether of people or objects, goes deeper and is more widespread, happening even in small village communities.

And while these Akan states developed, what was happening elsewhere? In the north the Empire of Kanem, greatest in the thirteenth century, began to break up; the capital was transferred to the rich lands of Bornu, west of Lake Chad, and there survived for many generations, a pastoral people ruled by capable warriors who finally imported firearms and became, for their own period, completely 'modern'. Yet the sixteenth century Idris Alooma, the importer of guns, was killed by a hoe, only weapon of some desperate farmer who saw his people attacked by the slave-hunters. For Bornu had begun slave-hunting campaigns in the south; the victims went to the markets of Tripoli and often on into Europe. Nor was this all their wealth. Under Idris Alooma, the empire of Kanem-Bornu spread right across Africa from Darfur in the east to the new Hausa states in the west. There were embassies in the north African capitals and even in Istanbul. There was an administrative system, offices, law and

Fifteenth to sixteenth century

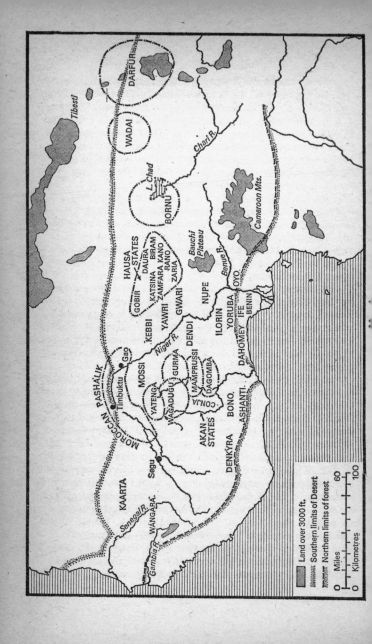

order, with the taxation necessary to keep up a court, a civil service and an army. There is no reason to suppose that all this was any less efficient than that in most contemporary European states. What appears to be missing is Shakespeare, Breughel and Leonardo, Copernicus and Galileo. Or is it possible that artists and scientists did exist, but their products have totally disappeared? Or, just conceivably, that they were unacceptable? If so why?

We must remember that these states did not have the kind of boundaries we know today, with fences and gates and customs barriers. The boundaries marked on the map are only approximate. The real boundaries depended on the strength and capability of the king and his army.

South-west of Bornu were the fertile plains of Hausaland and a series of small states. These were the people who developed industries, growing cotton, weaving and dyeing it, famous for iron and leather work. Their walled cities, Kano, Katsina and others, are solid monuments of trade and civilisation. They were adventurous people too, leaders of caravans on the longest trade routes. But they too were slavers, raiding their neighbours to the south.

One must of course realise that in all these states there were slaves who were not, normally, sold outside. They were part of ordinary society with rights and duties, and could usually rise in the social scale and become vassals of their masters, with land and slaves of their own. Or else they were skilled and valued craftsmen or soldiers of the king's army. People had not yet evolved a cut and dried theory of liberty. But that was something very different from catching slaves to sell.

Of the two main states which claim to have been born at Ife, Oyo was the biggest, a country where one could use cavalry; its borders cannot be drawn with any certainty; there was always conquest and readjustment going on. And in the process of becoming an empire Oyo took and sold enough slaves to makes itself prosperous. But to begin with, Benin was in the better position for the new slave trade—the trade with the ships rather than the caravans. The kingdom of Benin stretched some 250 miles along the coast, west of the Niger delta. It was the obvious place for European visitors to land, to be courteously treated and en-

quire about trading prospects. As far as Benin was concerned
it looked as though constant warfare would provide plenty of
material for trade. There would also be some other tropical products. But, for the early traders, Benin itself was an impressive
town with its great broad main street, going straight on for four
miles, with cross streets, all equally straight and surprisingly broad
to Europeans used to the narrow, winding streets of mediaeval
towns. Strangers might not penetrate far into the king's court,
with its galleries and towers, its pillars plated with bronze plaques
of battles and triumphs. But they could admire the king's horses
and note that 'he has also many gentlemen, who when they come
to the court, ride upon horses'.

The Obas, that is, the kings, of Benin in the Middle Ages
were directly representative of God or gods; their doings were
not counted as morally answerable to man's judgement. They
must be approached as though by a worshipper, although in practice they consulted a council of elders and had a hierarchy of
attendant nobles. The Obas or their priests used thousands of lives
to build up a structure of terror and power. Theirs was the first
African state which the Portuguese, courageously exploring round
the coast of Africa in their small ships, met and traded with, at
first mostly in gold, ivory and some spices, not so well marketed
as those from the East Indies, but profitable all the same. A few
slaves might be shipped to Europe, but they were not the main
traffic.

The Portuguese were at that time a nation who carried their
religion with them. No doubt the people of Benin were quite
pleased to introduce one more God in the general company
of gods; they already knew the new God's symbol, the cross,
since this was the tree coming up from the earth, the place of
the gods and the dead, crossed by the level road of man's life.
Nor would the idea of a crucified sacrifice for redemption or
purification be at all difficult to assimilate. The missionaries may
have felt at first that they were making progress, but not, perhaps, for long. However, Europeans were well advised not to stay
long on the coasts of Guinea; fevers of various kinds swept them
off. Safest, perhaps, to bargain from their ships.

Further west than Benin and Oyo lay Dahomey, another military state. This was an inland kingdom, originally a tributary of

Oyo, but it broke away and gradually conquered down to the coast where at first other states, which have not as entities completely disappeared, took the cream of the foreign trade. All these wars meant a certain number of slaves for sale with the ivory and gold, but, as the slave trade grew, not enough.

Six

The Slave Trade and What It Did

The harm which the slave trade did to Africa is almost impossible to assess and in a sense is still going on. The harm which it did to Europe and America is more measurable. The good which its apologists claimed for it either never existed except in their imaginations, or could have been achieved in other ways. Perhaps the only admirable thing that has come of it is the mixed civilisation of South America and the West Indies, which has already given the world a few outstanding writers, as well as a special brand of music, cricket and magic. We do not know, however, what was lost in the Caribbean Islands when the Indians, the original, gentle inhabitants, were exterminated. This happened almost immediately after the Spaniards discovered gold there and also discovered that the Indians stupidly just died when made to work fourteen hours a day, in mines or rivers, getting this same gold, lashed whenever they stopped. Negroes, they found, could stand it.

Here in an African town, living close and affectionately with my fellow tribesmen and tribeswomen, I can hardly bear to think how my white forebears—though not, I think, any direct ancestors—would have considered my friends here as merchandise, hunting out such texts as would excuse this profitable point of view. I think how they would, if they could have got at them, have loaded my friends, men and women stripped and tied and beaten into submission, terrified of being boiled and eaten by the furious whites, on to slave ships in conditions where the loss of a certain percentage of the cargo was considered only reasonable. At the final loosing of shackles in Kingston harbour, say,

some of these slave ships lost some of their best-priced goods because the slaves deliberately leapt into the sea and were drowned.
It was very annoying for the owners. But the slaves escaped into
death and perhaps a return to the ancestors. I think my friends
too would have leapt overboard. But luckily in slave-trading days
they were too far off, protected by too many natural barriers.
They have never been slaves or slavers, and because of that there
need now be no guilt between us.

Yet one must look at the slave trade sensibly, realising that it
was not all the doing of the Europeans or, later, the Americans,
and that, but for this trade, it might have been much longer
before Africa got the important American food plants which
in a sense, enabled the population to keep up in spite of the loss
of thousands of young men and women every year. Slaves had
been a recognised trade commodity all over the world before
the days when machines took over their hard and repetitive work.
But what made the difference in Africa was the scale. Never before had twenty million people—some say more—been treated
with such complete ruthlessness. Millions have been killed in
wars, more millions have died in famines or epidemics. But someone was sorry for them, tried to help them. The slave trade, as
it developed between West Africa and Brazil and the West Indies,
and later with North America, was something so deliberate and
so horrible that it has no parallel in human history.

It did not start from nothing. For centuries there had been
small-scale slave-trading going on along the north-eastern coast
of Africa, which developed later on into a regular export from
Zanzibar to India. Ever since the days of Rome and Carthage
some slaves had been sold into Europe from North Africa, often
involving long and painful marches. After the great Sudanic
states had dwindled, that trade still went on with their successors
who mostly got their slaves in war or raids on people to the south
of them. And there was always a slave trade with the Arab world
east of Egypt; we may as well remember that this trade still goes
on, illegally and horribly, though on a small scale. But so long
as some kinds of people are very rich and much less basically
civilised than, say, my friends in Mochudi, and so long as they
want to own human beings and be able to do absolutely anything to them, then other people will be found willing to do the

dirty work and take the risks of breaking the laws, without having any scruples about it.

And again there was slavery of a kind over most of Africa, as indeed there was over the rest of the world, but slavery modified in various ways, as we have seen. Prisoners of war, for whom slavery was a better alternative than death, were often assimilated or freed after good service. Certainly it would have had its risks: at Benin and doubtless wherever else there was a powerful god who had to continue to seem powerful and to be almost infinitely feared, to the great benefit of his priesthood. Here from time to time there would be immense and terrifying human sacrifices, the shrines would run with blood, and probably most of the victims would be slaves. (See Chapter 15). In general slaves would be outsiders, not 'us'. It would be 'we' who would become strengthened and feared. Sometimes this would be a slaver's excuse: he was saving people from a terrible fate so that they would be able to lead a useful, industrious life on a sugar plantation and even be baptised. But most slavers didn't bother with excuses.

The first Portuguese sailors and traders were not interested in slaves. They were full of the tremendous passion of curiosity, which was one of the great gifts of the Renaissance to Europe. They wanted to see round the next corner. Diaz rounded the Cape of Good Hope in 1488. Vasco da Gama came ten years later and though other countries would soon dispute Portuguese trade mastery, notably the Turks, for a time the Portuguese were the only Europeans whom any African was likely to see. It is always Portuguese soldiers, with their curious noses and beards, who are shown in the Benin bronzes.

The Portuguese began by having friendly relations with the Kongo. The Manikongo, the chief ruler, had a state under him which does not correspond to the modern Congo, but was large and prosperous. Subsidiary kingdoms owed him at least theoretical loyalty, and the Portuguese treated him completely as a royal personage and were in return well treated. The Kongolese royal family took easily to Christianity and sent sons or nephews back to Europe for education. One of these kings, baptised as Affonso (his real name was Nzinga Mbemba) ruled as an enlightened and energetic Christian for nearly 40 years. But during these years relationships with Portugal changed. The sugar plantations of

Brazil were being developed, Europe was clamouring for sugar. Portugal needed slaves shipped over to develop the sugar industry, since, again, the native Indians just died like fish in a bucket when made to work plantation hours and pace. King Affonso had been willing to trade prisoners of war in return for European goods, but this was not enough. He was less willing to sell his own subjects. Portuguese 'aid' which like some 'aids' in the present day, had strings attached, began to come to an end.

The next phase shows a Portuguese *conquistador*, Paulo Diaz de Novais, establishing himself at Loanda and starting a series of wars aimed at supplying the slave trade. His African 'allies' were carefully trained for just this and the southern Kongo was usually the target. One after another of the Manikongos, Affonso's successors, genuine Christians some of them, appealed vainly to their Portuguese fellow monarchs and to the various Popes. Nothing came of it. In a final disastrous war in 1660, the Bakongo were defeated, heavily enslaved, and the Kongo kingdom crumbled to its doom. Christianity for this independent African state was over, only perhaps mourned by a few missionaries whom the traders and soldiers doubtless thought of as poor fools. This was the beginning of the Portuguese occupation of Angola, which goes on still. Angola was used for two centuries as a source of slaves, and little else. This is not good for a country. If freedom fighters in Angola today control large areas of the country, it is due to terrible memories and the hatred of Portuguese methods which are fixed in the minds of ordinary Africans.

But this was not the main slave-trading area. The Spanish and Portuguese gold mines and plantations in the West Indies and South America were being steadily supplied with their labour requirements, mostly at first through Portuguese traders and in Portuguese ships, from the west coast. Often there was a mass baptism of the cargo before the ship sailed. But this could not last. The other maritime nations of Europe were bound to come into this new and obviously profitable trade. Captain John Hawkins, the first English sea-dog to go pirating down to the west coast and get himself a cargo of slaves 'partly by the sword and partly by other means' was first reprimanded by Queen Elizabeth. But shortly afterwards she went into partnership with him, and ¹⁵⁶⁴

granted him a coat of arms with a 'demi-Moor' chained, as his crest. Indeed the English royal house took an active interest. James, Duke of York, brother of Charles II, was in it in a big way: the slaves caught by his chartered company were handsomely branded DY.

The Kings of Spain, however, made the largest and steadiest profit out of the trade. They had a system of licences with strict conditions of numbers and price, and these licences were eagerly snapped up by people of many countries, but at first the slaves were all carried by Portuguese ships. For a time they had the trading monopoly, but this was broken, first by the Dutch, and then by the British who had by this time got their own islands in the West Indies as well as plantations in North America. The Danes came in on this too, though the French had thought out for themselves another area and were established on the lower Senegal. The early trading forts were all leased from whatever coastal kingdoms had control of the country between the Niger delta and later Calabar and Benin. They paid a heavy rent and were dependent on the local king's goodwill. And they were probably looked on as useful sources of power and luxury, bringing in quantities of acceptable goods, cloth, metal or wire, above all guns, and, later on, gin. These guns were of course essential for getting the main merchandise these strangers wanted: slaves. In fact there was a constant struggle going on along the west coast for possession of the actual coastal strip with these centres of splendid trade, and this struggle in turn produced prisoners for sale. Though when there were not enough prisoners people were constantly being caught in other ways, charged with lèse-majesté or offending the gods or spirits. If you were in power you couldn't lose.

Looking at it from the other side, it certainly did not seem conceivable to the British colonists in North America, for instance, that they should ever be able to exploit the natural resources of this vast country without slaves, and the Red Indians were very unwilling to be enslaved. The only people who did not accept this necessity were the Quakers, or some of them. The alternative to Negro slaves was of course white slaves or indentured servants. We should not forget all the Scots and Irish prisoners sent overseas by Cromwell and others, the kidnapped children and girls,

Barbadoe'd (as the phrase went) from Bristol and other ports. On the voyage over they were perhaps even worse treated than their black fellow slaves and were sold in as shameful and revolting conditions. Sometimes black and white slaves would run away together; the notices advertising rewards for recapture show this. But, unless they were used as straight plantation labour, they had rather more chance. There was not such an obvious demarcation line between master and servant; they probably went to church together and their children were not considered slaves. It was customary to set them free after a period of twenty or thirty years. At first indeed it was customary to free some of the Negro slaves, but they probably remained as servants. Later that custom dropped as the black slaves came to be considered by their owners as entirely chattels. They were children of Ham destined to perpetual slavery; the Bible had put its seal on it. They were not really human.

Let us look for a moment at the figures. During the seventeenth century the number of Negro slaves landed in all parts of America was getting on for three million, but in the golden age of the eighteenth century it must have been seven million and for the first half of the nineteenth century before the abolition of the slave trade, when the Yankee slave traders successfully dodged the British fleet, another four million were landed. But this represents only those who arrived alive at the other side. Perhaps another million for every four million either died or were killed on the way to the selling point in Africa or on the voyage, and that is rather a lot of human lives.

Most of them came from somewhere near the coastal regions, though a few had been driven from the interior, walking or being made to run hundreds of miles, carrying burdens, tied neck to neck or in forked sticks in the long, horrible slave coffles, silent or screaming. At the coast they became merchandise, bargained for between the kings and traders of the slave coast and the captains of the slave ships or factors of the on-shore factories. They might be kept in close, dark imprisonment for days or months in the barracoons, strong prisons into which they were thrown, or in the dungeons of the slaving ports such as Elmina. Then they were driven down across the sand towards the sea which they had perhaps never before seen and the pitiless Atlantic surf, thrown naked and tied into the surf boats and taken out into the ships.

There were two theories of shipping slaves. The loose-packers thought they lost fewer by giving them a few inches more room apiece. The tight-packers getting them in like sardines, thought that, although they had more losses, they did in fact make a bigger profit. And that was all that mattered. A slave was just whatever his or her weight of flesh would fetch in cash. If during the voyage they became worthless through sickness or accident, they were thrown overboard like spoilt meat. And naturally there were always epidemics, dysentery, smallpox and so on, as well as the fact that some of the slaves would not eat the food provided, especially horse beans, the cheapest fodder of all, not even when their mouths were forced open and their teeth broken.

All one can say is that the slave cargo, having a certain value, was sometimes better treated than the free crew, who, if they became sick or in any way unable to carry on with their duties, were flogged, starved or tortured at the captain's orders. No doubt there were some decent captains, and each nation accused the other ones of particular kinds of cruelty or—more often—of commercial double-dealing. But, as was said at the time: 'It is unaccountable, but it is certainly true, that the moment a Guinea captain comes in sight of this shore, the Demon cruelty seems to fix his residence within him.' In fact, it seems impossible to be in this trade and remain completely human; to have absolute power over other people corrupts absolutely. That is as true for a slaver as for a Roman Emperor. Let me quote again, from one of them: 'Some people may think a scruple of conscience in the above trade, but it's very seldom minded by our European merchants.'

There have been many books written about the slave trade and its horrors; there is no filthy thing one can imagine that did not happen in real life. All of us now condemn it. We cannot imagine how civilised people took it for granted, as they did, cultured Europeans of the Age of Enlightenment. Of course they had, most of them, not seen it or heard it or smelled it for themselves, and things at a distance are seldom real. But could their nice, happy world have gone on without it? Many fortunes were made out of sugar, shipping and tobacco; many splendid architects, painters, landscape gardeners, were paid out of these slave-made fortunes. The Government too found useful channels of taxation. How often in history have people willingly given up the sources of their prosperity?

But let us not be too complacent. The slave trade has left behind a residual feeling among Europeans towards Africans which is still at the back of all colour prejudice, making decent relationships between the white continents and Africa far more difficult than they would have been otherwise. There has never been quite the same social difficulty between Europeans and Asians, and this is not merely because Europeans know, or should know, that India has a very ancient civilisation. There were African civilisations, but Europeans were so unprepared to admit this that they sometimes destroyed the evidence (as at Zimbabwe— see Chapter 8) and always insisted until quite recently that there were none. Indeed it is only lately that a few historians have begun to disentangle and rediscover these civilisations; I am glad that so many of them are British or French, two of the old slaving and colonialist powers. But their work has barely got down to the level of schools. Stupid whites in all countries still feel that the black is a natural slave, an inferior: they think, deep down, why aren't they still slaves? And, on the other side, the American descendant of slaves finds himself hating the white descendants of masters, however much they may be on his side. I think we must all, black or white, watch ourselves carefully to see that no taint of slave-trading is left in us.

Seven

Slaves and Slavers

On the African side, slave-trading was equally debasing, though perhaps less horrible. The African king or chief and his go-betweens or caboceers, or the African private trader, had nothing to do with the Middle Passage: the stinking holds full of bruised, chained bodies: the daily 'dancing' on deck, a piper and several whippers in attendance, until chained ankles bled into the scuppers from the harsh bounce of the iron: the battening down during storms, when the ships' surgeons, trying to patch up such broken bones as would mend, had to go barefoot over packed bodies while half-mad slaves bit at their feet: the sales where the plantation owners rushed on board to seize the likeliest goods. The African chiefs and traders had nothing to do with plantation punishments. They merely had to organise the supplies and to drive as hard a bargain as they could. Yet they must have been fully aware of the cruel cross-country drive of the slave coffles, hands chained, necks in forked branches, where the loaded women were made to throw away worthless babies. These were their fellow Africans. In the long run, perhaps this betrayal was worse than anything the whites did.

The current rate for slaves might be in copper bars or in tobacco or linen handkerchiefs. Sometimes cotton cloth might be the best currency, but guns, cutlasses, gunpowder and knives were always welcome. In some places cowries were demanded. All depended on supply and demand. The ships' captains would also no doubt have to make presents to suitable people. Laced hats went down well, but again, muskets and powder were the real thing. Often brandy, rum (another produce of the West Indian sugar plantations) and gin eased a sale.

One result of all this was that other trade dwindled, or was not built up and encouraged. There was some sale still for ivory, and of course gold, but the supply of gold had slowed down. The predominance of the slave trade was one of the main things which stopped any development for production in the African towns or states. It also of course checked any kind of peaceful development, since war and what it brought was so obviously profitable. One side of the trade could not have gone on without the other, and what corrupted the white corrupted the black. Indeed it was worse when a chief sold his own men or rivals. It broke the sense of tribal cohesion and order on which people depended. Nobody was safe : everyone was afraid. In this atmosphere the worst kinds of magic flourish.

Slave supplies meant constant wars and raids and a constant state of stress with one's neighbours, who might hit back, however much one was armed with the guns and cannon of one's sales. The reason the Ashanti confederacy went in for large-scale conquest was to get at the profitable coastal markets, to sell their Ga and Fanti neighbours (who have perhaps not quite forgotten it) to the Portuguese, the British or the Dutch, playing them off against one another.

Oyo intended to cut out Benin and ended by succeeding; a great deal of the trade was transferred to Lagos. The small states, little more than sprawling trade towns with a bit of land behind them, of Andra and Ouidah, which became notorious as Why-dah, were based entirely on slaves. There was no other industry. The king of Whydah was so suspicious of the whites that he would allow them only a mud fort on an island three miles from the shore.

But Dahomey managed to crush out the smaller states and take on the trade. From the fifteenth century on, several states had established themselves in the network of rivers which makes up the Niger delta, usually with a good trading port as their base. Some were offshoots of Benin. The most important were Brass and Bonny. By the eighteenth century their whole reason for existence was the slave trade. There must always have been some background of farming, but the rulers always thought first of trade. Naturally the Europeans followed the politics of the coast with great interest. If they got it wrong or backed

the loser, they might easily get themselves killed, often un-
pleasantly.

Not that life was anything but precarious for Europeans who
landed on that coast. They died of one fever or another, and
this was to go on until comparatively modern times, when it
began to be understood which insects carried the fevers, and
how epidemics could be checked. They were frightened at the
back of their minds all the time and took it out of anyone who
was in their power. The smell of the mangroves breathed death
at them as soon as they came near shore. One 'factory', typical
of many, stood 'low near the marshes, which renders it a very
unhealthy place to live in; the white men the African company
send there seldom returning to tell their tale. 'Tis compassed
round with a mud wall, about six feet high . . . a most wretched
place to live in, by reason of the swamps adjacent whence proceed
noisome stinks and vast swarms of little flies, called Musketoes
which are so intolerably troublesome that if one does not take
opium or laudanum 'tis impossible to get any sleep in the night. . .'
And while the drugged sleeper snored the anopheles mosquito
would have passed on the malaria.

There was social life of a kind, though naturally no white
woman would have ventured out. The kings and 'campashiers',
who were the actual salesmen, had to be visited. There, for instance, was the King of Whydah on his throne 'raised about two
feet from the ground and about six foot square, surrounded with
old dirty curtains . . . with a bottle of brandy and a little dirty
silver cup by his side; his head was tied with a roll of coarse
calico and he had a loose gown of red damask to cover him; he
had gowns and mantles of rich silver and gold brocaded silks,
trimmed with flowers of small party-coloured beads . . . but he
never wore shirt, shoe nor stocking in his life'.

The King of Whydah seems to have been notorious for cheating, palming-off old slaves or sick ones during the inspection that
went on before the branding and shipping. But there was talk
of other things besides trade. I quote again, from the mid-
eighteenth century: 'You'll find men of ready wit in all things
relating to common business, yet if they guessed concerning a
future state they give up all pretentions to humanity and wander
in absurdities as black as their faces.'

From time to time some king or chief would try to stop the whole thing, saying that slaves must not be taken through his dominions, but this was easily circumvented. If there was a shortage of Africans for sale, it was easy to kidnap or 'panyar' them, either through agents or by putting a ship's boat ashore. Children fetched quite a good price and were less troublesome than grownups. Another method was for a ship to lay out attractive goods on the deck so as to entice visitors, who would then be carried off. But usually there was a war or a raid sooner or later, sometimes between close neighbours like the old and new town of Calabar.

A slaver's surgeon, for instance, reports in his diary : 'No Trade yet but our Traders came on board to Day and informed us the People had burnt four towns of their Enemies and indeed we have seen great Smoke all the morning a good Way up the Country so that Tomorrow we expect Slaves . . .'

How could a country ever develop when this was going on all the time? How was civilisation ever to come into existence, since civilisation implies some settled law? How was any kind of moral order to survive this? It was always the handsomest and strongest, the cream of the community, who were in demand, though sometimes this made trouble : occasionally the slaves managed to revolt and kill at least some of their captors before they were—almost always—overpowered themselves.

One can see something of what kind of people they were, even from the reputations they had with their captors; there were the Mandingos who were farmers from Senegambia, often large slave owners themselves, no use as plantation slaves but good house servants; there were the Krumen, sailors and fishermen, very powerful, seldom enslaved, though later they took to the sea and were thought better than many a white sailor. It was the Krumen who ferried the slaves across through the surf with tremendous skill and strength, and perhaps still keep the monopoly in many ports. The Gold Coast slaves were much esteemed by those who could tackle them; they were the leaders in slave mutinies, but also, for the rare owner who could learn to make a friend of a slave, they were 'not only the best and most faithful of our slaves, but really are all born heroes'. One wonders if these 'Coromantees' were really Ashanti; the description seems to fit.

Then there were the Ibos and Yorubas, known as Nagos.

There were all the mixed tribes from round Calabar. When a tribal group managed to keep any cohesion or when, at the far end of the voyage they met others from their own country, they redeveloped whatever national habits their masters allowed them to have. The immensely complex myth world of the Yoruba, which one sees in Amos Tutuola's books, transferred itself to Brazil or Haiti, picking up whatever seemed suitable in the Christianity to which most of them were introduced. In general, such things as dances or any religious ceremony were strictly forbidden by the masters, on pain of death or worse. Things forbidden tend to go bad in the darkness; gods become evil spirits, religion becomes magic.

Meanwhile cotton was becoming the great plantation crop. And cotton goods from England were clearly going to outsell Indian cottons so long as the price could be kept down. Invention after invention made the cotton industry of Lancashire. It sometimes seems odd that nobody thought of working the English cotton mills with slave labour; perhaps they did. Perhaps the only reason it didn't happen was that English men, women and children came to the mills to work for little more than it would cost to keep a slave and in conditions almost as bad as those of slaves. The only ones who were flogged much were the workhouse children; but under-feeding is also good for discipline. Slaves were not needed. And the Abolitionists did not always notice what was happening in their own country.

On African slavery, they won. It was partly that decent people in Europe and America just could not stand the horror any longer. The Quakers, as so often since, were the first to do anything practical. They formed an association 'for the relief and liberation of the Negro slaves in the West Indies and for the discouragement of the slave trade on the coast of Africa'. However, the American Quakers, nearer to the real thing, had begun to denounce slavery as early as the end of the seventeenth century. Others joined in; English writers, religious and political leaders, the Vice Chancellor of Cambridge and especially William Wilberforce. In France the revolutionary humanists came to the same conclusion as the British Christians.

Denmark forbade traffic in slaves in its possessions after 1802. Other countries followed. From the end of the eighteenth century the slave trade was being discussed and going through the leisurely English parliamentary procedure. But although Britain ended the trade officially in 1808, it was still some time before so profitable an activity could actually be stopped. Gradually, however, all countries agreed to put an end to the trade with Africa, though slave systems went on for much longer in various places, including of course, the southern states of America.

1833

But what happened in Africa itself with the ending of the slave trade? Clearly it was not received with joy by those who had profited by it there and who did not find it shocking. The first place to be seriously affected was West Africa and especially the states which were entirely keyed to the slave trade. These states were as independent as the city-states of Greece or mediaeval Italy; they had their quarrels. In the four Calabar states one curious thing united them, the Egbo Society, which was partly religious, partly designed to keep order and decorum, but mostly to protect the interests of the rich. The kind of protection may be gathered from the fact that Egbo means Leopard. Its activities went everywhere; in the diary of Antrra Duke in 1785, the Egbo Society keeps coming in, sometimes when there is a sharing out of initiation fees, sometimes when a trading dispute is taken up by Egbo. In 1807 when Britain withdrew from the slave trade the business men of Egbo must have called furious meetings invoking power after power, completely unable to understand why their old trade partners were drawing back.

In that same year, the King of Bonny, equally taken by surprise, spoke for himself and his council of elders and chiefs: 'We think that this trade must go on. That also is the verdict of our Oracle and the priests. They say that your country, however great, can never stop a trade ordained by God.' How this must have surprised some of the good English abolitionists who sincerely felt that their humanitarian legislation was bound to be equally appreciated in Africa! It is not the last time that the export of some kind of Western idealism has not worked out as expected.

Certainly the oracles (in Professor Onukwo Dike's translation), the blood-stained idols (according to the missionaries), or the jujus, (as most Europeans recognise the word), were very important. The slave trade, coming south along the Niger, was controlled by a network of city-states there, of which the most important was that of the Aro people, who were called the Children of God. This was because their shrine was acknowledged as a sacred centre all through the delta and beyond. It established, through fear, veneration or what you will, a kind of trading-peace and also a court of justice that was much more powerful than the justice of any kind of state. Further, those found guilty by this court, had to pay a fine in slaves. If the guilty ones were a large group or clan this would be a hefty fine. These slaves were in theory 'eaten' by the god, which no doubt accounts for the fact that the British destroyed the 'Long Ju Ju' in 1900. But of course they were in fact traded down the river to Bonny or another delta port.

The Aros were an Ibo people, and the Ibos have always been extremely successful at organising trade and at adapting their methods to changing circumstances. That does not always make a people much loved by their neighbours, especially if their neighbours are somewhat backward looking and afraid that their own power and prosperity may suffer. History is full of variations on this story. The Ibos were among the first of the west African peoples to adapt themselves to the surprising new conditions which the end of the slave trade brought.

It must be remembered that meanwhile the trading cities were organised in 'Houses'—great trading households, often consisting of thousands of people, free and slave. But here the slaves attached to the Houses were not mere chattels, especially if their fathers were freemen and their mothers slaves. This put them a step up the ladder and they had a far better chance of ending up in good positions and freedom than the children of free fathers and slave mothers in America. For all, bond or free, the head of the House was 'Father' and he rewarded good work. The House was a complete trading organisation, perhaps with its own war canoes, heavily armed from the goods which the English traders had brought. A successful House, in the Delta states or the Calabar states, would have thousands of pounds passing through its hands and a heavy investment, partly in buildings and equipment, partly in money lent to merchants elsewhere. The heads of the Houses found the British attitude extremely difficult to understand, especially because at first the Portuguese, French and others went on saying what a good, and God-approved thing the slave trade was. No doubt it was more difficult now that British squadrons patrolled the seas just beyond the ports, and it was certainly a worse risk for the slaves, since a ship carrying slaves was liable to be seized. If there were no slaves on board it would not be seized. So, if a slaving ship was hard pressed, rather than lose the whole thing, the captain would dump his cargo overboard. Better five hundred drowned slaves tied to the anchor chain, than a valuable ship taken by the British navy.

The African middle-men just couldn't make it out at all: the kings and chiefs, and the heads of the Houses sold prisoners, criminals and occasionally slaves who belonged to the Houses but were disobedient or idle. Why did their old friends the British want to ruin them? Above all they were passionately against letting any white men get beyond the coastal region, beyond their own monopoly, and into trading relations with the people further inland. It was only a few of them who realised that they must think up an alternative. There were fewer elephants now, less ivory. Gold was harder to come by. Spices were better produced in India. Timber was wanted but the trade had to be organised. But there was one commodity, palm oil, which could be substituted and which came from much the same part of the country as many of the slaves. Europe was taking to washing in a big way—and with soap. The new engines, on railways or in factories, had to be greased. In three years between 1827 and 1830 imports of palm oil to the United Kingdom, though still small by modern standards, had more than doubled. But there was another side to this. A new set of British traders had realised that they must get to the hinterland of Africa; here would be the new material and here, they hoped, as habits of industry spread, would be the new markets for their own manufactured goods. These men, some of whom were the successors of the slave traders and working from the same ports—Liverpool for instance—had their representatives in the British Parliament. The anti-slavery group, too, realised that there must be an alternative trade.

This will be picked up again in Chapter 15 with the story of Ja Ja and the rise of Opobo. We have followed the west coast slave trade to its end and must now turn to other parts of Africa.

We must, however, first note how trade, and especially trade in
African raw materials, became linked up with the ideas of explorers and missionaries. The explorers genuinely wanted to explore; they were passionately interested in finding the source of
the Niger and the other great African rivers. The first of them
was Mungo Park. The missionaries genuinely wanted to bring
Christ to the heathen, to teach and to heal. But none of this was
possible without financial backing. This came from the commercial interests, at home. The man on the spot was MacGregor
1808-1861 Laird, who put all his strength, all his considerable intelligence
and push, and all his money—he lost most of it on one expedition
but that didn't stop him—into the great adventure of Niger exploration. Sometimes he brought in the name of England (or
Scotland) and civilisation, but usually he talked in down-to-earth
terms of trade. And by trade, men like MacGregor Laird meant
trade on equal and decent terms with African fellow men with
whom they would be in a commercial relationship, at least, of
mutual trust and respect.

Eight

The Boiling of the Pot

So far we have been able to follow in some detail what was happening in west Africa. We shall go back there. But meanwhile how were things going in central and eastern Africa? It is quite certain that there was continual movement within the region by groups of people with different customs and speaking different languages. Sometimes they came peaceably, but more often fighting and raiding. This went on for centuries and is to some extent remembered in tradition, but tradition is not always accurate. People alter it so as to produce a better impression, or so as to make out that their own beginnings were very important—that they descended from some god perhaps—or else that they are really related to this or that still more important group. In the boiling of the pot all round Africa, we find tribes and clans from north and south, conquering one another, simply absorbing those whom they have conquered or sometimes keeping them permanently as social inferiors. This is something which may work out all right for the conquerors for centuries, but not for ever. And the worse the position of those who have been kept down, the worse the ultimate revenge.

Some of the groups who came up from the south were distinctly savage. There were the Zimbas in the sixteenth century who moved up the east coast, where, as we have seen, there were prosperous trading cities and a good deal of wealth. Some five thousand Zimbas fell on these towns 'killing and eating every living thing, Men, Women, Children, Dogs, Cats, Rats, Snakes, Lizards, sparing nothing'. But the people moving in from the north were probably not cannibals. They were rather lighter in colour and tended to have a more elaborate type of ritual, initiation ceremonies and organisation. But very little survives of what they made and did, unless some of the songs and music. Some owned cattle and drank the milk; others owned cattle and ate them; each group must have found the other strange and perhaps blasphemous. If your tribe had one kind of initiation rite, you would not feel that your neighbours, with another kind, were really clean or adult.

Throughout central and eastern Africa there are enormous earthworks, and probably many more still forgotten and buried in jungle or marshes, about which little is known, except that it must have taken a great deal of social organisation to get them built. There are ancient remains of elaborate irrigation systems in the Kenya highlands; nobody is quite sure who made them, but parts are still good enough to be used. And then there is Zimbabwe, the kingdom which we only begin to know about when it was already in decline.

We do know that there is a large area in southern Rhodesia in which stone ruins can be found; one of these is the great Zimbabwe. It is not built with any kind of architectural skill; the walls are roughly built stone, without mortar. But the Zimbabwes are strong enough to have outlasted the centuries and there are strips of diagonal stone decoration as well as loop-holes for arrows; the masonry is thoroughly competent. But the builders had not yet even thought of an arch. The greatest is like a reed fence palace and defensive earthworks translated into stone. We would of course know much more about it, but that Rhodes' followers, about whom we shall read more in Chapter 13, were encouraged to take any gold they could find: this is the more shocking because it was already in the days of archaeological interest. However, it is unlikely that Rhodes' men were interested in history—in any case they put down the Zimbabwes to mythical 'civilisations' from the pseudo-European north, being unwilling to suppose that Africans could have built them. And the gold objects, which museums now would give their ears for, were probably hacked up and melted down. Let us not, however, forget the worse destruction of the Hellenic monuments and especially the Parthenon, by equally uncaring Venetians and Turks, or the Pheidian statues ground to powder by Moslem peasants intent on the destruction of 'idols' or broken up and sold as souvenirs to nineteenth century tourists—and lost as completely as the Zimbabwe cult objects. For that matter let us not forget the destruction of exquisitely beautiful Christian statues and cult objects by the zealots of the 'Reformation'. Probably this kind of thing is still happening somewhere in the world.

We do know that the king who ruled over this state in its later years was called the Mwenamutapa and his people were the Makaranga : but of course these names have been Europeanised. It seems not unlikely that they were the ancestors of today's Bakalanga, though also, no doubt, of today's Shona peoples. They imported and wore cloth from the east coast which they had exchanged, probably for the usual ivory and gold. It seems also that the Mwenamutapa was a priest-king and that much of the organisation of rule depended on his falling into a state of possession, probably by the ancestors, and especially at new moon. There was a court with an elaborate hierarchy which we hear of from early Portuguese observers. There was a sacred fire and the dead king's soul went into the body of a lion. He was probably the intercessor between his people and Mwasi, the spiritual being embodying social justice and order, whose followers, later on, in the 'Mashona rebellions' were killed as witches and centres of disaffection. It seems then, that Zimbabwe was at least a settled state, and that some civilisation had developed there, in fact that it had developed and elaborated, but did not have whatever quality a civilisation must have in order to grow, to take in new ideas and at least some kinds of technology. A society that does not grow is fairly certain to be destroyed as soon as it meets one which is growing and it does not seem as though the Makaranga had any kind of efficient military organisation. Nor had the Rozwi who were probably the earliest inhabitants and who were subdued, but later came to dominate this central empire.

In fact the kingdom of the Mwenamutapa, whatever dynasty was in power and whatever groups broke off or became incorporated, seemed to become increasingly dependent on the Portuguese. They retreated towards the north. Other states rose around their borders. In the end they were destroyed by Ngoni coming north after the *Mfecane* in the early nineteenth century; the stone Zimbabwes were captured and the people broken up or absorbed by their conquerors.

Here we should stop to notice the word *Mfecane*, which will come into this book increasingly. It is a Nguni word for the wars and movements of people which followed the rise and expansion of the Zulu empire. These were hard times, as bad perhaps, as the European Dark Ages when, again, whole peoples were scattered and displaced. But it means something different in the minds of those who use the word. For southern Africans it means a period of breaking and violence, but also of glory, even if you were on the wrong side. It is something to look back on with pride.

Most of today's larger African nations include groups who are different in language, culture and looks, as different as French and Italians, say, but much smaller in numbers, though not smaller than those nations were in the early Middle Ages. There are other groups which are not so separate, whose language and customs are as alike as Northumberland and Lancashire. Most of the larger groups and some of the smaller ones, have histories going back for centuries. These histories tend to be fixed (as English history was when I was a child) round royal families, their feuds and battles and good or evil deeds. Much of this may also involve religious cults which have been disapproved of by missionaries and branded as causes of disaffection by white rulers.

Only a wise African ruler, who really wants the good of the whole of his people, can make these groups into a nation without damaging them and perhaps destroying part of their history. Luckily, such heads of state exist. In an earlier economy it might have been possible to allow these groups (which one can call either nations or tribes according to one's political philosophy) to work out their own destiny as similar European groups did. But modern technologies appear to demand large numbers, capital beyond the reach of the African individual or small group, and a very expensive infrastructure of administration, transport and so on, which can only be provided by the larger unit.

Meanwhile, the history of the Bantu states in central Africa, north of the Zambezi, is somewhat uncertain, both on area and on dating, but we do know something of the economic basis.

The Katanga country is not only rich in easily worked copper, but consists of open forest with reasonable rainfall and good rivers. These are excellent conditions for settled civilisation.

There were salt pans; and, the more heat makes people sweat, the more they need salt. The Luba and Lunda people had worked copper for many centuries and progressed to iron; they defended themselves, hunted and traded; they made handsomely decorated and burnished pottery; they had ornaments of copper wire. The Lunda kings, probably in the divine tradition, had courts where skilled craftsmen were working until the end of the nineteenth century. They could import what they wanted both from east and west.

The Bemba state to the east of the Luba, was later in coming to power and was probably based rather more on trade with the Arabs. Further south the Lozi of Barotseland had a complex system of administration, based on the special economy of the flood-plain in which they lived. They had an elaborate judicial system and managed to hold together, in a loosely defined area, a number of different ethnic groups. One must also remember that before these various groups came in and settled there had been a few wandering people, users of iron, hunters and tillers but not organised into states. They were probably absorbed.

Still further to the north-east it was the same kind of story. Between and around the great lakes there were the beginnings of kingdoms, varied in origin and language. It was fertile country and attracted invaders. Some of these racial variations still persist. Nor is it always the conquerors who end on top. Here was order and a comparatively settled life of herding or agriculture and crafts. Yet all round them and through them there was always a continual movement of people, usually but not always in peace.

But why did all the people who did not settle go on wandering? It may be that cattle increased too fast for the land to be able to feed them, especially if none were killed and eaten, and people's lives had to be adjusted to cows. The fertile earth, when it had not been disturbed for many years and humus had accumulated, had only to be scratched for crops to come up; they did not take many months to mature. And again, the climate did not make it necessary for people to build strong, warm houses. However, in time a process of conquest did stabilise a few kingdoms; there had to be some kind of centre of power if you were to hold down and claim tribute from others.

Gradually the kingdoms between the great lakes began to take shape, the southern ones of Rwanda and Urundi and the Ugandan states. Here the first and most important was Bunyoro, with Buganda as one of its sub-kingdoms, which, however, was watching for the moment and marched in on Bunyoro in the mid-seventeenth century. This went on, until, in the nineteenth century, Buganda had annexed most of Bunyoro and had itself established a strong centre with considerable trading interests and consequent wealth in imported goods. The Kabakas of Buganda organised royal bodyguards and also a system of state officials dependent on the Kabaka's pleasure. They wore imported cotton from India, ate off Chinese porcelain and wore copper bracelets. They had also by this time discovered that almost labour-free but also protein-free crop, the banana.

Uganda is still a country of magic and possession. The hill shrines of the dead Kabakas are still potent. One comes to the threshold of these superbly shaped thatched palaces of the dead, past guard houses and palisades : the history is recited by those for whom it is more real than the present, those who are half-identified with their ancestors. In the intricate windings behind the bark-cloth arras anything may be happening. Death is unimportant so long as the correct rites of passage take place. Here, as in Zimbabwe, the new moon is the time for trances, for closest contact between dead and living. People are drums and drums are people. All this gives an alarming sense of strength, of a social structure which Europeans find difficult to deal with, unless, that is, they are prepared to use brute force to destroy it, as they have done so often in similar positions. For the whole apparatus of magic is as materially easy to destroy as it is difficult to get rid of. It may be better to come to some compromise, as Columba did with the Celtic gods and goddesses, turning them into saints. From the Anglican cathedral, drums, not bells, call to prayer; perhaps they are the voices of martyred Christians.

This atmosphere met the early explorers. For, by the beginning of the nineteenth century, there was hardly any part of Africa which had not had some kind of contact with some kind of white men, or was not about to have it. It may have been a remote contact, yet there was a spreading outward of echoes of what was happening in Kongo and Angola, which after the Portuguese had

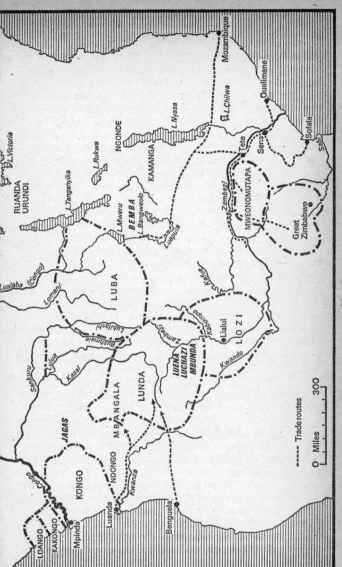

Map 5

used it for a slave supply-base for Brazil, had lost any sense of African moral order. But further up the great river complex of the Congo were other kingdoms, loosely organised, the main one being the western Lunda state whose rulers were called Mwata Yamvo. They were mostly in the ivory trade, and what they wanted in exchange was guns and gun-powder.

For some at least of the southern Congo tribes, the forest, the place of magic, was loved rather than feared. It was the mother that gave food, above all, meat and honey; it gave shade against the sun. There was always excitement in the forest, and the spirits of the forest enforced good relations in the community, as they do still among the Lele people.

Probably the forest pygmies have not altered their way of life for a very long time. Why should they? After all, they appear to be enviably happy, loving the forest and in a good relation with it which appears, in some way that cannot perhaps be put into rational words, to be mutual. They have escaped most of the fears and jealousies which make life miserable for so many people; they can afford to be kind. And for centuries they have not wanted what they did not have. According to Western ways of thought this is shockingly unprogressive; I am not so sure. At the moment they seem able to get certain luxuries through their relations with the Bantu villagers. Of course if they can be grabbed for taxation to pay for things which they do not want, like roads and police, they will be hauled out of their Garden of Eden.

Meanwhile, the western seaboard kingdoms had been broken up. The savage Jaga, fiercest of the central groups, had attacked the Kongo kingdom, already weakened by the Portuguese. But they went on to attack (and perhaps eat) the Portuguese and in alliance with Queen Nzinga of Angola, stopped them from spreading much beyond the coast. However, between the Portuguese and occasional other invaders coming from the sea and the Jaga from inland, the administration and culture of Kongo and Angola broke down completely. The Portuguese conquerors had little interest in what lay to the south. It was a dry, parched country, but even so the Herero grazed their cattle there and there were groups of Khoikhoi (whom the Dutch, later, called Hottentots) and Bushmen, still in the main hunters and food gatherers. But the Herero and Khoikhoi took a crop wherever they saw a place where there had been good rains. Then they moved on. From Angola down to the Cape it was never empty country, but the populations were never static.

Between the great lakes and the east coast, the country seems to have been reasonably settled, a fairly fertile country of small villages and patches of cultivation. These were usually cut and burnt scrub which would then bear a crop for a year or two before the fertility ran out and the land had to be left. But there were always a few better bits of country where one might find permanent gardens and bigger villages. There was some hunting and trapping, a few cattle, enough drink to keep away worries. There might be trouble with slave hunters from time to time, but in the main there was peaceable exchange, hospitality to strangers, perfecting of old skills—here an elegant form of house-building, there iron-casting and welding—but no change, no history.

Further across, the whole of the east coast was dotted with trading ports and small towns, some on islands, which was rather safer, though the prosperous island of Kilwa was attacked by hosts of the Zimba who killed, and presumably ate, several 1585 thousand of its inhabitants. These ports were valuable possessions and were struggled for, through diplomacy and war, by Portuguese and Arabs, ending with a predominantly Islamic culture. But this was all on an African sub-structure. The Swahili language began to develop throughout what was known as the land of Zanj. Up to now we cannot say exactly how this important but historically recent language started. We do know, though, that there are many Swahili manuscripts, in poetry and prose, still in existence, but not yet either printed in Swahili or translated. It may be that the poetry will be found to have Persian influences, for the charming practice of the *mushira* existed: where a room of poets sit round, a candle in front of the one who is reciting, but all savouring and repeating the best of the lines. Probably, too, there were wandering bards singing the praises and deeds of noble families, as they did in ancient Greece in the days of Homer.

In the richer houses there would be silken hangings or imported carpets hanging from the walls, and there would be handsome rugs for those who sat out on the *baraza,* the shaded platform in front of the house where men gathered—and still gather—for important discussions. People might eat from Chinese porcelain and their food was now more varied, thanks to Portuguese imports from South America of such things as maize, cassava, cashew nuts, guavas and avocados. At night, in times of trouble, the houses would be shuttered and shut fast by splendid doors, studded with brass nails, such as one sees still in Zanzibar and some of the coastal towns.

Map 6

Their slave trade had been negligible up to the eighteenth century, though no doubt they had household slaves, probably traded from the interior, along with foodstuffs, ivory of course, copal and ambergris. But in the eighteenth century they too became involved in a big way in the slave trade. The French in particular came in on this, but found that the local sultans insisted on so high a percentage of the price of each slave, that it barely paid. Gradually Mombasa and Zanzibar came to be the main slave trading centres, and, though the Sultan of Zanzibar agreed in 1822 not to sell slaves to any of the Christian powers, the slave market there went on much longer for India and still more, the Arab countries.

And further north? After the Arabs whose original thrust had taken them deep into Spain, were thrown out, there was a general Christian assault on the Maghreb—the northern coastlands of Africa. From the fifteenth century on, more and more Mediterranean and Atlantic sea-ports fell to Portuguese and Spanish expeditions. In fact, most European maritime powers joined in. For these were all rich and prosperous cities, probably as full of beautiful buildings and gardens as anywhere in the world, and of course splendid for looting, extraction of heavy ransoms and the usual forcible conversions, as well, of course, as the release of Christian captives.

However, by the sixteenth century the Ottoman Turks were an up and coming power, not only conquering much of eastern Europe, but pushing west along the Maghreb into a series of tributary states, largely corresponding with the present ones. The Turkish governors were on the whole sensible and co-operative; trade and agriculture were encouraged, order upheld. The Moroccan west remained independent, finally recovering the lands conquered by the Portuguese.

The Ottoman Turks now occupied Egypt, but did not make any move towards conquest further south. We know little of Abyssinia, now called Ethiopia, the successor state to Axum, in the early centuries. The rise of Islam cut off its old contacts with the Mediterranean world, yet for a long time there was no war between Moslems and Christians. The sultanate of Funj lay to the north but Nubia remained Christian; the states of Darfur and Wadai, nominally Moslem but perhaps basically pagan, lay to the west. Down through the Middle Ages, Abyssinian pilgrims, thousands of them, came marching north through Egypt to the Holy Lands, welcomed there by their Coptic brothers, flying great flags painted with saints and crosses, beating drums and conducting a Christian worship which would have seemed highly heretical to the narrowly regulated churches of Europe before the Reformation, and perhaps even worse after it. The Patriarch of the Monophysite Church came from Alexandria, but lived in Cairo; there must have been much peaceable coming and going. Saladin, the great romantic figure among the Moslem Defenders against the Crusaders, in one of his gestures of generosity, gave the Abyssinian Christians a church of their own in Jerusalem.

But the real danger to Abyssinia or Ethiopia as we now call it, was from the south. The country was invaded and partly laid waste, but a dynasty of heroic kings, leaving their ruined capital for tents and spears, led a resistance which was to end by the conquest of the southern, pagan people. Later they attacked the neighbouring Moslem trading states on the Gulf of Aden and so provoked a *jihad,* a holy war, by other Moslems against Ethiopia. Meanwhile, they had built some wonderful churches; art and imagination were on a Christian sub-structure, but became more and more definitely Ethiopian. Further excavations and researches will throw still more light on this.

Sixteenth
century

No doubt Ethiopian echoes came south into the rest of Africa. Indeed it may have been Ethiopian conquests to the south which set going some of the waves of migration which in time met the other waves from the south. But, after a period of expansion, Ethiopia began to break up again. A large country without adequate transport or communications is always likely to do that, especially if the centre concentrates too much on its own interests and importance. If railways and telegraph lines had existed in the time of Alexander's Empire or the even wider spread Roman Empire, they might not have fallen to pieces; nor might the Sudanic states of Kanem or Songhai.

For by now these great, loosely held together empires of western Africa had largely broken up. This was partly due to the Moroccan invasion of Songhai, though the main result of this was to form a new upper class—the users of firearms. Later the

Late
sixteenth
century

Mande subjects of Songhai set up a number of small states, which were to last, more or less, until the Moslem conquest in the early nineteenth century, which was in turn attacked by the French a generation later. The French were established in the small trading port of St. Louis (the old capital of Senegal) and from there they moved up the Senegal river, which they had soon realised would be the great trading highway into the interior. 1857

Rivers were important ways of communication. Kept clear and with steam boats which could make headway against the current, they were as useful as railways. Nowadays we think in terms of transport planes and wireless, but the old-fashioned methods would have been good enough. The first steam engine was invented in Alexandria two thousand years ago, but was only considered a toy, just as the Chinese invented explosives, but only used them for lovely fireworks. So far human inventions have been developed only for war or money or occasionally art. It is only in the last hundred years that we have begun to think in terms of health and increasing the world's food supply, and then mostly because the advanced people are afraid that great numbers of others who are ill or hungry are a danger to them, and will, for that matter, not be able to buy what they have to sell. From the very beginnings, Christianity (and all other great religions) have bidden us feed the hungry, comfort the afflicted, love and not hurt. One of the greatest merits that a Moslem is enjoined to acquire is the freeing of slaves. But it is in the Moslem world that there is still slavery, and conditions perhaps worse than slavery exist for the 'Indians' in Catholic Brazil.

Yet perhaps at last and driven to it by H-bombs worse than hellfire, we are beginning to think in terms of humanity as a whole; this advance in moral attitude has been largely made by scientists and historians of all countries and colours, who perhaps can see a little further into the future than the rest.

Nine

Beginning of the Frontiers

The Dutch had an important trading company in India and the Far East, in the days when governments were not interested in imperialist expansion themselves, but encouraged trading companies, such as, for example, the British East India Company. Such trading companies were sources of vast European riches and patronage of the European arts. In the mid-seventeenth century the Dutch company planted a small colony at the Cape, half-way to their East Indian goal.

People had just begun to realise that fresh vegetables and meat kept sailors healthy. Citrus fruit was known to cure scurvy which might lay low a whole ship's crew. Fresh water, too, was essential. Soon this extremely beautiful country, this potential Garden of Eden, became a place of convalescence under the strict supervision of the Dutch East India Company, the V.O.C. The first little settlement was entirely for supply and health purposes, but was gradually joined by others, including some groups of Huguenot refugees, who went in for more varied horticulture and agriculture and meant to stay permanently.

Naturally, there were other people there when they arrived. These were the herders, brownish yellow people, speaking a difficult language full of clicks, who pastured cattle, goats and fat tailed sheep. These were the Khoikhoi—the Men of Men—but the Dutch called them Hottentots. There were also hunters, with bows and poisoned arrows, the San who were called Bushmen. At first all went smoothly; the Khoikhoi were quite pleased to trade their cattle and occasionally to work; there was plenty of land. But such idyllic conditions do not last long. Soon the colonists had pushed out beyond the first fences, taken land for large farms, begun to cultivate vines and better types of stock and to go in for business, sometimes slipping through the tight monopolies of the V.O.C. They began to import slave labour from Dutch Batavia in the east as well as from other parts of Africa and Madagascar. There were few white women, and Malaysian girls were particularly beautiful. But the Khoikhoi began to find themselves being crowded out, they and their cattle driven into worse land. What did it mean, anyhow, thought the Africans, for one man to say he owned the land—the land which, like the air, belongs to no-one and everyone?

There was no good land wholly unoccupied anywhere in Africa. The herders wandered. So did the hunters. The women of both people found roots, eggs, fruit, small game and so on. Both were very partial to wild honey. If any of them went over the hills to the north-east they found taller, darker people, speaking another language and with a different breed of cattle, the Xhosa people, also on the move. To the north-west too, if they moved far enough there was another Bantu group, the Herero. But deserts and mountains lay in their way. Why must they go so far?

Meanwhile the white colonists were becoming increasingly dissatisfied with the Cape and passing ships as their only market, above all with the strict controls of the Dutch East India Company, the V.O.C. They took to smuggling when possible and demanded a larger share in the government. The Company was not always sympathetic. New experiments were constantly being made, but factories and new agricultural methods usually failed; there was cattle disease and smallpox which, incidentally, devastated the Khoikhoi when it got among them. During the eighteenth century colonists began to move out further, hunting, trading and cattle farming, not always troubling to build a house but living in their waggons as 'Trek Boers'. Relations with the Khoikhoi became worse. The San, the Bushmen, thought of water holes essentially as good hunting grounds and were highly displeased to see them used by the white men's cattle. Bushmen, to be sure, had poisoned arrows, but a rifle had a longer range. Most farmers would have been delighted to see the Bushmen completely exterminated, as the Tasmanians were in the early nineteenth century. Women and children, when not killed, were 'apprenticed'. This was the word for slavery: perhaps more accurately slavery over a period of ten, twenty or more years. It was also tried out on English boys from the Refuge of the Destitute, a kind of work-house, not very successfully. In the end the Bushmen were pushed out into worse, drier and wilder country, where it was hard for them to survive, where indeed they only did so because nobody else wanted their land.

To some extent the Bushmen, the San or Masarwa, are, like the pygmies in the Congolese forests, on good terms with their natural environment. But many of them were made into serfs in the nineteenth century by the incoming Batswana, themselves pushed out of better land by Zulu, Ndebele and Boer pressure, and for the rest, the Kalahari is not as kind a parent as the central forest, and, if it can be improved, the Bushmen are in danger of being pushed out again, unless they agree to settle. Their future may be in gradual absorption and, of course, the loss of their highly developed skills especially in hunting and water conservation, useless in a world of technological progress, and yet a triumph of man's ingenuity in the face of nature. Although much of their dancing, singing and apparently effective methods of curing remain, they seem already to have lost their ability to paint as brilliantly and directly as their ancestors did; perhaps for that it was necessary to have more confidence and joy than they have now.

There is one rather curious thing which has been traced back to one at least of the forty burghers who colonised the Cape and who now have at least a million descendants, including of course a number of Coloureds. This is the 'porphyria' gene, which shows up very clearly in the individual who carries it, partly as a skin condition and partly as a tendency to psychological disturbance which may be triggered off in various ways. With this gene latent or apparent among a good many of the million descendants, there may be some physiological accounting for some present-day South African attitudes and difficulties.

The slave system, even under relatively mild Cape conditions, still had its bad effects on slaves and slave owners. Enormous slave brothels were kept for the sailors and it was from these that the cholera epidemic, which decimated the Cape, started. In the mid-eighteenth century Van Imhoff writes: 'Having imported

slaves, every common or ordinary European becomes a gentle-
man and prefers to be served . . . the majority of the farmers in
the Colony are not farmers . . . but owners of plantations and
many of them consider it a shame to work with their own hands.'
So social attitudes start. But plenty of inter-colour marriages
went on all the time.

The dispersal of the migrant farmers, the 'Trek Boers', also
went on, heading increasingly east and north east, crossing one
river and mountain range after another, looking for higher rainfall and better grass. However, grass, especially *sourveld* grass,
good in early growth, but useless later, has to be managed.
Herders, moving on, are a natural form of management. But
when people settle, with cattle as their wealth and main crop,
it is easy to overgraze and this may mean permanent damage to
the pasture. During the treks whole families moved, taking with
them their household goods, their indentured servants and slaves,
Coloured or African, and their religion, including an unswerving
belief in themselves as the Chosen People—a belief which kept
them going through danger and sickness—but little in the way of
education for their children, other than Holy Writ. In fact they
cut themselves off from the intellectual progress which was going
on in Europe and America and which touched the urban Cape.
The ox teams plodded on. Then, on the other side of the Fish
River, they met, not dispersed or dispersable Khoikhoi and San,
but organised Bantu nations. And this meant war.

Nobody knows for certain through how many centuries Bantu
people had been gradually spreading southwards from the Zambezi. There are, for instance, air photographs of *kraal* circles
scattered over the Transvaal, including the Reef District, which
is now claimed (though only by politicians, not by reputable historians) as never having been African-inhabited country. It is
not clear how old these circles are and it is sadly certain that
widely varying interpretations will be put on them and on other
evidence of African occupation. From another angle, African
oral tradition may well not take account of dates, being more
interested in the run of the story and the people involved. History,
when not pinned down by documents and artefacts, is a rather
tender plant, and in many parts of Africa it is liable to be distorted by political considerations. Most of the written evidence

from early European sources, is naturally enough about the coast.

What is certain is that, by at least the seventeenth century, perhaps earlier, Nguni groups, that is, people speaking some version of Nguni, had been moving into and settling in the fertile lands to the west and south of the Drakensberg range, along the Caledon and Orange River valleys and again, between the range and the sea, always spreading further and further south (see Map 7). From the foothills they could see their cattle grazing, great glossy beautiful herds, moving where they chose, the herd boys guarding and guiding them, the kind land giving them grass for health and increase. This increase of cattle meant also the increase of people. A bride was courted with cattle for her family; cattle meant pride and feasting.

The people of the Nguni chiefdoms were strong and healthy too. They ate meat and much milk. They got plenty of wild vegetables, roots and fruit from land which was still uneroded, fertile, giving its best. A man can work and fight and grow to his full height and strength on such a diet. When, today, he is only given mealie porridge short of vitamin B2 and such scraps as the white housewife can spare, he may work after a fashion and in a way to cause considerable grumbles. But he tires easily. He cannot be himself. Perhaps that is the idea.

There were other Bantu groups and nations, speaking languages fairly near to Nguni, though with fewer or no click sounds. The Sotho people were mostly further north and west; they tend to have different customs and kinship systems. We know little of their early history. People have forgotten who built some rock forts, now deserted, or when or why. But it looks as if most of the Sotho people lived north of the Orange River and south of the Limpopo and gradually spread further west and across the Marico to anywhere that looked like good grazing and hunting ground. The Venda were mostly further north across the Limpopo and the Tsonga along the northern coastal lands. No doubt there was some intermingling, groups breaking away and being absorbed by others, so that one can only now guess what happened by slight differences of speech and custom.

Meanwhile, there were wars in Europe which involved British and Dutch. In the late eighteenth century the British took over the Cape from the V.O.C. which ceased to exist, and stayed there for eight years. After that it went back to Dutch rule under the new Batavian Republic. Then, following the Napoleonic wars, it came back to the British who remained there, while the uncertain borders of the colony moved north.   **1815**

Probably this made little difference to most of the people whose allegiance changed, but they continued to press for more say in the government. British rule meant rather less trade restriction, rather more tolerance, rather more European culture coming in. And in time it meant more insistence on some kinds of social justice, ending in the emancipation of slaves and abolition of near-slavery such as the 'apprenticing' of children. It also meant an increasing cultural division between the mainly English speaking towns and the countryside where people spoke a kind of Dutch, the 'taal' which was to develop into Afrikaans. This in turn produced an unacceptable and unpleasant upper class mentality among the English, which has not been forgotten or forgiven by the descendants of the burghers and Huguenots.

The English government found the Trek Boers a considerable nuisance, difficult to control, behaving uncouthly, involving the authorities in frontier incidents. But for the Nguni people they were something worse. For generations it had always been possible to move on. The herds increased, the wives had babies, the sons of one house in a great *kraal* would take whatever they needed and drive their cattle on, amicably or sometimes not so amicably, leaving the rest of their families. Then they would build themselves a *kraal* in a fresh bit of country near a river or spring. All would begin again. But now? If they crossed the Fish River they met these fierce, red-faced, bearded men with the guns. By what right should the Fish River not be crossed? Among the Nguni it was the ama-Xhosa who asked that first.   **1779**

They were used to fighting. It looks as if there had been continual minor warfare of one kind and another all across southern Africa, probably depending less on people and rulers and more on whether or not there had been enough rain for grass to feed the cattle. Besides, what else of interest was there for men to do during winter? It varied from family bickerings in which few people lost their lives, and which could often be settled either by single combat or by lengthy and enjoyable law-suits, to large

scale migrations of whole tribes and their cattle, wiping out whoever stood in their way. This might lead to total devastation of
huge areas of land—yet if there is rain how quickly land recovers
in Africa—and indiscriminate death. Younger sons of chiefs, or
elder sons when the state marriage to the Great Wife (through
whom the succession to the chieftaincy came) had been made late,
broke away or murdered their brothers. Small quarrels were
fanned into large ones that ended with burning of crops and
kraals, temporary alliances with other chiefdoms, and the minds
of the men on little but war: not only the men, but women like
Manthatisi, the fighting queen of the Batlokwa whom one of
the French missionaries described as an intelligent woman with
a sweet and agreeable expression; no doubt she was happy to be
so efficient a leader. Yet war, after all, when not taken too
seriously—and quite often it was an affair of champions and
ransom—was an alternative to sport, which occupies so many
men's minds, equally fruitlessly, though less destructively, today.
A warrior had plenty of delightful opportunity and looked extremely handsome; a good fighter was probably an equally good
dancer. But it was a continuous waste of talent and energy. If the
southern African people had been left alone to develop, would
they have settled into more permanent towns or villages, taken
more interest in agriculture, trade and finally, the arts? Would
they have dropped the emphasis on war? This appears to have
been the sequence in other cultures, in Africa and elsewhere,
which started as hordes of warriors (although another possible
sequence is to take war so seriously that you must start thinking
and acting in terms of science and technology). It seems likely,
but not inevitable, that this would have happened in southern
Africa too. But in fact, with the coming of the white invaders,
they were put into a position where the warriors were still the
most important group in the community and the bravest and
cleverest fighter was the natural leader.

But, before the coming of the Trek Boers tribal movements
were not necessarily a matter of bloodshed. When people saw
their cattle, as well as their wives and families, threatened, they
often just moved on. There were no walled cities or even forts to
act as defence places. There were few material goods, not much
more than a few strong women could carry on their heads. And

there was always ungrazed land somewhere. But this meant that there could be no elaboration of culture into buildings or artefacts. There could be little development of new techniques except in fighting. There was no place to stay still and think, no civilisation. This was the beginning of the *Mfecane*, the period of breaking and dispersal of the tribes, corresponding to the European Dark Ages. And the real enemy was coming up from the south.

In and around Natal, and south again between the Fish River and the Drakensberg range, chiefs and their followers had begun to turn on one another seriously, fighting for grazing rights instead of being able to move on. Sometimes these wars were rather formal; a gallant enemy who had surrendered might be incorporated in your own tribe or ransomed for cattle. But towards the end of the eighteenth century, a baby boy was born among the Nguni, who was going to alter all that. He was an unwanted child, begotten in carelessness, not for a long time acknowledged by his father. He was given a shameful name. But he was to make it a great and terrible one. His name was Shaka.

Meanwhile, Africa was in the news. All over Europe gentlemen in frock coats and uniforms were lecturing and writing about it. It had hold of people's imagination; it came into poetry and painting. Explorers and travellers began to work their way in, usually up the main rivers. They were backed by interested groups, not entirely approved of by governments, since this exploring might involve them uncomfortably; there was no great rush towards empire in any European country; they were too busy dealing with the problems of the industrial revolution.

One notices among the early travellers a very friendly attitude which was almost always reciprocated. There was for instance, the charming king of Karagwe in East Africa, whose hospitality so delighted the English explorer Speke. 'He was alarmed, he confessed, when he heard we were coming to visit him, thinking we might prove some fearful monsters that were not quite human, but now he was delighted beyond all measure with what he saw of us.' Speke and Rumanika spent many happy days together, in gentlemanly pursuits, for of course the English upper classes always get on well with their own kind of whatever complexion. They could relax behind the screen of grass plumes in elaborate iron holders, which have only recently been found again. There was much conversation. 'I explained to him how England was formerly as unenlightened as Africa, and believing in the same sort of superstitions, the inhabitants were all as naked as his skin-wearing Wangambo; but now, since they had grown wiser and saw through such impostures, they were the greatest men in the world.' Happy Speke! He was probably too busy making preparations for his expedition while he was in Europe, to notice the hauntings of a spectre. But the Communist Manifesto had already been published, ten years before.

It does seem true that, wherever Europeans and Africans approached one another in an unaggressive way, they always seemed to get on well, believing as much or as little as they chose of what the others said. Of course there were also aggressions on both sides, fear and misunderstanding. Above all, perhaps, there was what to African eyes was astonishingly bad manners and peculiar behaviour by the Europeans, especially towards those things and persons which were thought and felt to be sacred. Much was allowed for, but certainly some African peoples were too quick on the draw; others had suffered so much from the slave traders that they were understandably suspicious. I can understand the kind of thing that might have happened; if among the Tswana peoples, some white missionary or explorer had been honoured by having a Praise shouted at him, the manic rapidity of which sounds to a European ear only aggressive, but is really an incitement to further admired action, it might have scared him out of his senses. He might have reached for his gun.

If, however, the white man happened to meet one of the essentially predatory tribes, who saw everyone as their natural prey, things were often less pleasant. So they would be if the Africans they met had only seen or heard of the whites as slave-raiders. This was so for the French and British missionaries who came into the parts of Africa where the Portuguese had been before them. And one must also consider how very unpleasant the first sight of whites must have been, the dreadful blue eyes, the horrible beards or body hair, the limbs for some frightful reason enclosed in bags. Children often ran shrieking away from the most kindly disposed traveller.

But the main enemy for Europeans, especially on the west coast, was still the various fevers, though the use of quinine to some extent eased the malaria situation. And again, you were likely to meet lions or leopards or be charged by a rhinoceros when you least expected it. Africa was a challenge. Above all, perhaps a challenge to the churches, where heroism was beginning to come back into its own after a century of Vicars of Bray. And this was to be heroism on behalf of others, of an inaccurately imagined, but very vivid, 'darkest Africa'.

For there had been a sudden rise in faith and works in the various Christian countries of Europe. They had stopped fighting one another and the energy which had gone into religious wars was now going outward. Most of the Protestant missions, starting with the Moravians, were formed during the eighteenth and early nineteenth centuries. The Church Missionary Society was founded in 1799. Others were taking shape, first in Germany, a generation later in the Catholic countries, though, once they started, they went ahead vigorously. Yet it took time for misssion work to start; plans must be made, money collected, the right people recruited. And while this was going on, the potential missionaries were themselves living in a society where there was increasing talk of industry and markets and spheres of influence. All over Europe it was a society which was steadily growing richer, even if the riches were not justly distributed. But the dogma that the industrious, the thrifty and the sober were, under manifest providence, inheriting the earth, was part of accepted social doctrine. And this was to be a main export to Africa.

The Missionary Society at the Cape, Dutch and British at first working together, went into action in the last years of the eighteenth century and founded Bethelsdorp, where Khoikhoi and Coloureds came increasingly to take refuge. They were safe there from soldiers and masters as well as those who corrupted with strong drink. The missionaries were not popular with those who preferred things as they were. John Phillips, born in 1775, was the son of a Kirkcaldy weaver, in many ways a typical stiff-necked disputatious Scot, for the Gospel and 'agin' the Government. He held the heretical belief that 'Hottentots and Kaffirs', and especially perhaps the Griquas, could think and work and gain salvation in complete equality with whites. More heretically still, he thought of them as potential consumers of goods, if once they had the money to buy them. This kind of thinking tends to put up the price of cheap labour. Phillips and like-minded men in the London Missionary Society were much hated and abused but refused to give in.

They were also to some extent a reflection of the British attitude towards 'the natives', which was a quite kindly one, based on the eighteenth century idea that all men are brothers. Those who hate this idea say it is only held by well-off people who live at a distance and know nothing about the practical problems. The trekkers would certainly have said this—brave and tough-minded men like Potgieter, Pretorius and Retief who led their followers out of the interfering new-fangled laws and ordinances of the Cape Government and well away from the missionaries to where, as they would have felt, a man could be a man.

Islam, too, was making converts, gradually spreading down east Africa in the wake of the traders, but more quickly in west Africa. Most of this was due to the Fulani, who were much influenced by a series of religious revivals. Devoted brotherhoods felt a sense of the danger in which Islam lay from the Christian up-and-coming north. Uthman dan Fodio came from the northern-most of the Hausa states and studied at the Islamic school at Agades, capital of the Tuareg state in the Sahara. He came back with new ideas of a militant and stricter Islam menaced by the general advance of Christianity and became a reformist teacher. But his main pupil, heir to the ruler of the Hausa state of Gobir, reacted against him. Dan Fodio retired, but became a centre for reformist agitation and, when his former pupil attempted to suppress this, he found himself proclaiming a *jihad* or holy war. The Hausa cities, thought of as corrupt and decadent, yielded. Uthman dan Fodio and his followers swept away many remains of the old Sudanic states, halted only in Bornu, and came south into Yorubaland and the Oyo country, bringing their doctrine with them. Once the holy wars were over, dan Fodio went back to his books, and the Fulani Empire was organised by his brother and his son. All was based on walled cities, fire-arms, orderly trade and regular hours of prayer. The trade followed the well-known routes, north to the Mediterranean, south to the coastal states and east as far as Egypt, or indeed to Mecca with the pilgrims.

For a time there was no clash with European interests. There

1754-1817

was still room for all. Denham and Clapperton explored from the north in the early nineteenth century, but neither they nor René Caillié, typically enough for a Frenchman exploring without government help or backing, nor the later German explorer Heinrich Barth, were in any sense a menace. They were infidels, no doubt, but they were received with courtesy.

By now the Portuguese had lost their old lead and vigour. It had come with the Renaissance, but the money values of the slave trade and a narrow-minded Church had almost destroyed it. Here and there Portuguese travellers and traders went inland and reported; their evidence is still very important. The Portuguese held onto the part of east Africa which is now Mozambique and onto devastated Angola. But there were not formally mapped out with fixed boundaries; they were, rather, spheres of influence.

But already the British Government was preparing other expeditions and this was partly due to the successor of the African Society—the Royal Geographical Society. Prince Albert was deeply interested. They must have mulled for months and years over maps of Unknown Africa, with those fascinating, tantalising gaps, before, in the mid-nineteenth century, they sent Burton and Speke to find Lake Tanganyika, and, later, Speke and Grant to the Victoria Nyanza and the Nile. But where would the source of the Nile turn out to be? The source of the Congo? Or the Zambezi?

Actually, the first European who set out to look for the Nile source was the usual crazy Scots laird; his name was James Bruce. Some of my own forefathers knew him well. That was in 1769. He went up the Blue Nile, found 'the Ethiopian Church completely Africanised . . .' Much was arranged by the priesthood in the line of organised miracles. Here he found himself thoroughly and enjoyably at home with an Ethiopian Court, which seems to have been about as savage and despotic as the contemporary Russian one, the attitude of the Emperor being much like that of the Great Catherine, who also liked having crazy Scots about.

He found quite a number of Greeks there, so that the link with the Mediterranean survived, tenuously. And in the end he was taken to the source of the Nile: 'as cold water as ever I tasted'.

It must have been an enchanting place in the hills. 'I came to the island of green turf and stood in rapture over the principal fountain which rises in the middle of it . . . though a mere private Briton, I triumphed here in my own mind over kings and their armies.'

He did not, however, try for the source of the White Nile, and it was seventy years later, in 1841, that a Turkish captain sailed well up the Nile. Egypt, now under the Turks, was going to come in strongly on exploration and the trade that went with it. But those who exploited the centre, the north and west, were not aware of what was going on in southern Africa. Dan Fodio had never heard of Shaka, nor would he have cared. He would not have been interested in King Nampoina of Madagascar, who founded the Merina state, and his successor who modernised his armies, thought in terms of economic prosperity, and who finally brought in Christian missionaries and started schools. Such people were infidels; he would not have dreamed of calling them fellow Africans; that was more than a hundred years ahead. No doubt North Africa, where his fellow Moslems lived, meant something to him. But the great distances had not yet been shortened.

Ten

The Heroes

If the Europeans were to be halted from occupying all south Africa it would be essential to have unity among the Bantu tribes, or, if not unity, a unified command. What you think and write of the men who, in fact, did this or tried to do it, depends on your point of view. If you believe entirely, or almost entirely, in the civilising mission of the Europeans: if, that is to say, you take it for granted that they are the 'goodies' and the Africans in consequence the 'baddies', then you cannot avoid making the usual historical judgements about Shaka, Dingane, Moshweshwe, Cetshwayo and the rest.

If on the other hand you do not see history in these terms, if you see that the wars which these men waged against the Europeans, are not over and done with: that in fact they are still going on: and that it is no longer clear that the whites (notice, I no longer say 'the Europeans') are always right, then you must take another look at some nineteenth-century African figures. Meanwhile it is as well for Europeans and Americans to remember that for several million Africans, even if they have been through schools where they are taught the Europe-orientated version of history: even if, in order to get through exams, they have described King Shaka as a blood-stained villain: these are yet the hero figures in their history. They are in the African background, just as other hero-figures, Caesar and Alexander, Charlemagne, Harald Hairfair, the Black Prince, the Bruce, Henry V, Ivan the Terrible, Cromwell, Napoleon, are in the European background. These were all fighters, military heroes, all of them responsible not only for splendid victories and sometimes for great national liberations and great ideas, but also and in great amounts, for death and cruelty and misery. That is the way of such heroes. That is the kind of hero Shaka was. In time we may have better African hero-figures: men and women who do not kill or conquer or torture, but give their lives otherwise for their own people and mankind. But the old kind of heroes are part of the structure of a people's history: cut them away at your peril. One day African poets and painters will show their heroes symbolically, transmuting all into another art form. But that has not happened yet.

Meanwhile we had better understand why certain men are in fact African heroes. Go back to the end of the eigteenth century and the unending minor warfare between different tribes or break-away groups of the Nguni people. Dingiswayo, of the ama-Zulu, understood the folly and waste of this; no doubt it was discussed in the great councils, but in terms of conquest. Yet the ama-Zulu were only, in numbers, one of the smaller chiefdoms of the Nguni people. And there was always fighting. Nobody had thought out any kind of permanent getting together; an alliance would be made, but might be broken almost before the hides of the cattle which had cemented it were dry. Yet conquest might be achieved without all-out 'red' war; Dingiswayo always believed that this was possible. But his young General, Shaka, did not think so, and when Dingiswayo insisted on sparing and making peace with his enemy, Zwide, head of the Ntethwa confederacy, another Nguni group, Shaka was perhaps sensible in counselling against such a policy. Zwide was an old-fashioned tribal conqueror, who only thought in terms of war and was never going to settle.

c. 1810

What we do not know is whether Shaka realised fairly early that an enforced unity, first under Dingiswayo, then under himself, was necessary if the whites were to be checked. What we do know is that, in his later years, he was well aware of the whites and the challenge that they were making; he understood, partly at least, their powers and their shortcomings. His relations with the trader and explorer Fynn, were always friendly, and he sent an embassy to enter into tentative relations with George IV, which was, in the event, stupidly treated, and achieved nothing.

It is possible too that Shaka and his councillors realised that, with the rapid increase of Nguni population, the old system of splitting up into groups moving off and starting new chiefdoms, was no longer possible. There was no more room. There must, instead, be central organisation and control.

Much is remembered about Shaka, but, as is the way with heroes, much also has been, and is still being, invented. We know that, like many other military geniuses, he invented a new weapon, the short stabbing spear, and perfected an army divided and drilled into impis, hardened by relentless training (in which he always took part himself) which was in itself an extension of the weapon. This corresponds to Philip of Macedon who invented the sarissa, the heavy Macedonian spear, and the highly disciplined phalanx that was drilled into its use. Or again, it corresponds to the English long-bow at Crécy, and the military formation that went with that. For a weapon is no use by itself, as is plain from the military history of tanks.

Much of Shaka's army organisation is curiously reminiscent of Sparta, even in detail, including the rules of celibacy for the young warriors, and the eating together. Perhaps there are only certain military disciplines and patterns which work, at any rate for an army which is not highly educated and in fact made up of technicians.

Shaka's first aim was unification; he saw that it had to be done by using himself as a symbol of absolute authority first over the ama-Zulu, then over other Nguni peoples and that this meant complete ruthlessness towards his enemies and the winning of every battle, however great the difficulties and whatever the losses to his own impis. It is possible that he also saw through this, realising it as a temporary necessity for people conditioned towards authority and war as the Zulus were. Had he lived longer he might have managed to alter it. He was warned against the dangers of absolute power, but could not accept the warnings; he may have felt that some day he would be able to accept them, but the day never came.

But, if you were competent, fearless and intelligent, you became his friend; it did not matter that you came from another tribe or that your beginnings were poor. If Shaka thought you were worth having he established you and loved you. He had a cattle selection and breeding policy; he thought about civil as well as military organisation. He broke the power of the witch-doctors, the smellers-out of evil-doers, who had kept his people in terror, and who, in a sense, challenged his own power. Whenever one finds that witch-doctors have real power it means that there is stress and anxiety in the community; Shaka could not have got rid of them without easing this and giving people the moral security that goes with order, courtesy, generosity and justice. But he did keep a war-doctor of his own, whom he consulted, much as Lars Porsenna of Clusium, in the poem, consulted his prophets who took the omens in the same kind of way as they were taken in Zululand. It is possible that some of the drivings and killings of the *Mfecane* were part of a deliberate policy of 'scorched earth' belts, between his empire and the whites.

It seems that Shaka was a man of strange moods and affections. He was curiously sensitive; he stopped some of the cruellest forms of punishment and death, though any breach of discipline in his army machine was punished by the quick club or spear. His mother, Nandi, who had loved him when he was a despised small cowherd, meant too much to him; he was so overwhelmed at her death that he did dreadful and insane things for a time. He refused to have children of his own, having had the bitter experience of being disowned by his father Senzangakona, although later on this same father was intensely proud of him. His love was for his step-father Mbiya. It is said that he was faithful, after a fashion, to one intelligent woman, who advised and warned him and was never jealous of his many court beauties. And again it is said that it was this woman who in the end kept the hyenas from his murdered and deserted body, ran miles across country to warn his friends that murder was coming their way too, and at last stabbed herself and died with his name on her lips.

Above all King Shaka had vision. He saw the waste and stupidity of tribal war and yet he knew that the only way to keep his people together was by war and the disciplines of war, outlet for Zulu arrogance and curb for individualism. It seems as though sometimes everyone grew tired of this and wanted to settle down. But there was always a new conquest to be made and young fighters and leaders to be tested and proved. Above all he gave the Zulu people, and to some extent the rest of the Nguni, identity and self-respect, so that they were able to face the new

European weapons and technologies and, later, to learn how to use them. He or his legend stopped millions of people from feeling that they were inferior, natural slaves.

One of these young leaders was Mzilikazi, The Great Path, eight years younger than Shaka, handsome and splendid, grandson of his old enemy Zwide, but his pride and joy. But he was one of the men who continued the miseries of the *Mfecane*, conquering and driving other tribes and making his own Ndebele into a great fighting nation. I, writing in Botswana, find it hard to call Mzilikazi a hero; he killed and drove my fellow citizens out of pleasanter, more fertile lands. Certainly he built up the Ndebele into military efficiency, but that, I think, was as far as his vision for them went, though he also enforced law, kept order and was friendly and hospitable to those who were not his immediate enemies. He was as responsible for death and suffering in Africa as Charles XII of Sweden (now one of the most peaceable and responsible nations of the world) was for the same thing in Europe. Is William the Conqueror a hero? Hardly, and yet he has a place of pride and honour in English history; the same kind of place may be kept for Mzilikazi. Another of the same kind was Sebetwane who led the combined tribes of the Makololo on a long and victorious trek northward, ending in Barotseland and the temporary extinction of the Lozi dynasty.

Zwide, whose own sons had been killed by Shaka and whose grandson had deserted to him, had another great fighter among his Generals. This was Soshangane who founded the Shangaan Empire, beyond Zululand. He defeated the Portuguese, as well as many of the Voortrekkers who came as far north as his country.

The time came when Shaka, ageing and reacting bitterly against it, partly in jealousy of younger men, began to lose the love and trust of his people. He was feared by almost all, hated by a few. It ended in conspiracy and assassination. His half-brother, Dingane, who may or may not have been one of the murderers, succeeded him as King of the ama-Zulu. The thought that he may have been one of the murderers has blotted his name in the minds of the Zulu, and his methods of dealing with the whites have blackened him in their history books. The danger was nearer than in Shaka's day and not to be met by playing British·

and Boers off against one another, nor yet by killing some of his most dangerous enemies, Retief and his men, after inviting them to a feast at which he had promised to sign away to them the whole of Natal. In this way he had got them to lay by their intolerably superior arms and dismount from their terrible horses. In fact the Boers were killed by the infuriated Zulu women. It may be remembered that Dingane allowed the English and American missionaries to escape.

Yet almost at once afterwards, Dingane's impis were beaten at 1838 the battle of Blood River and he was forced after all to cede Natal, and also to pay an enormous indemnity in cattle. He never saw clearly enough the long term and often distant politics of the whites to come to terms with them. It might have been possible with the British who really wanted a quiet life; it was not possible with the infinitely land-hungry Boers. It must be remembered, however, that King Dingane was a competent commander. Before the Natal affair he had defeated Mzilikazi and freed the Pedi people who had been held in near serfdom. After his death his brother Mpande was next in succession, and one of Mpande's sons was Cetshwayo. He was the last of the great Zulu tradition. His story comes into Chapter 12.

For a time southern Africa seems to have been divided and re-divided up by the white rulers in what seems now to be a very artificial way. Boundaries were adjusted by harassed and impatient soldiers and administrators, with missions coming in on the side of their friends or protégés. One of these nineteenth century countries was Griqualand, which started off with a series of tough and able half-breed chiefs and kept a degree of border peace. Trek Boers were not allowed to consider Griqualand as unoccupied territory. But elsewhere, wherever there was a rich valley, green grass and water, it was thought of as a free gift to God's own whites.

One part of African country after another became a battleground. Only the dry and difficult bits or the mountain tops were left. It was in the mountains that another African hero ruled, as bravely as Shaka and more diplomatically than Dingane. This was Moshweshwe of the Mountain of the Night, Thaba Bosiu, warm-hearted and generous, the founder of the Basuto nation. As a boy he had been marked out and advised by the

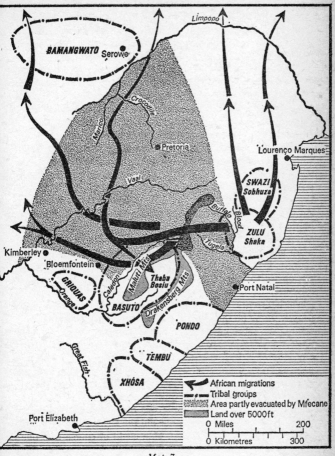

BAMANGWATO Serowe

Limpopo

Crocodile

Marico

Pretoria

Vaal

Lourenço Marques

SWAZI
Sobhuza

Buffalo

Blood

Kimberley

Bloemfontein

ZULU
Shaka

GRIQUAS

Orange

Caledon

Maluti Mts

Tugela

Thaba
Bosiu

Drakensberg Mts

Port Natal

BASUTO

PONDO

Great Fish

TEMBU

XHOSA

African migrations
Tribal groups
Area partly evacuated by Mfecane
Land over 5000ft

Port Elizabeth

0 Miles   200

0 Kilometres   300

Map 7

wise and gentle Chief Motlomi, the judge and rain-maker. Starting with a few hundred followers and gathering in the remains
of broken tribes, he had beaten off Zulus, Griquas and Ndebele.
He was intelligent enough to welcome the Paris Evangelical missionaries but not to be spiritually overwhelmed by them. He listened to their advice and saved much of his land because of it.
They upheld him when he claimed, rightly under Bantu law and
custom, that he could not sell land, either to the rival Wesleyan
Mission or to the Boers who had not moved on as he had intended them to do, but were settling on to some of the best lands
on the borders of his own country and Griqualand.

Moshweshwe claimed more land than he could probably have
held, but he had some support from the British Government,
with whom he remained on good terms. The British were meanwhile edging the Boers out of Natal and turning it into a British
possession. Gradually, too, they were edging in British Residents
beside the Chiefs. They would help in mixed trials between
African and white, and also help to keep the peace. And indeed,
by this time Basutoland—Lesotho—was beginning to have such
a reputation for peace, prosperity and good government that
more and more remains of broken groups came to join King
Moshweshwe. So long as Residents remained rather shadowy, he
put up with them. But when they tried the strong hand, he was
extremely reluctant to consent, and in fact the British lost his
friendship from that time on. However, this only interested a few
people. Most of the British on the spot were, understandably
enough, far more interested in the difficulties of coping with the
Trekkers. They in turn were becoming increasingly impatient of
any kind of British rule and were setting up constitutions and
organs of self-government. The British in mid-Victorian England
saw delightful visions of ever increasing riches, power and knowledge, and were torn to the quick by the miseries of their own
poor. Now that the slave trade was over, most of them could
not be bothered with Africa, nor did the fashionable economists
yet favour imperial expansion. One could of course ease one's
conscience by subscribing to a mission to the heathen. But it was
all too far off to be real.

In fact it was now becoming clear to the Boers that Britain
was unwilling to be firm and they had better come to terms them-

selves with Moshweshwe. There was some bargaining. All went reasonably well. Meanwhile the independence of the Transvaal was recognised by Great Britain whose Prime Minister was by this time Lord Grey.

By now it was becoming standard to say that all cattle which had been raided or which someone claimed had been raided, had gone to the Basuto. There was a sudden British demand on Moshweshwe for 10,000 head of cattle. A compromise was arrived at. Moshweshwe beat off a British punitive force. Some cattle were returned. Honour was sufficiently satisfied for the moment, on both sides. The king kept his cattle raiders in hand, no doubt saying one thing to them and another to the British, as national leaders under outside pressure always do. Nowadays we have speeches and newspaper 'leaders' designed to be read, sometimes by people inside a country, sometimes by people outside; the difficulty is that the wrong people sometimes read them! If your views are not set down on paper for anyone to see it makes things easier for a ruler practising diplomacy, as Moshweshwe was.

He was not the only one who had gathered up the remains of tribes and chiefdoms and built a nation out of them. Another was Sobhuza, who gathered those who had fled north from Zululand and built them into the beginnings of the Swazi nation. He and his son Mswati kept the Zulu military organisation but after his death there were quarrels. It was good land and of course white farmers and concession hunters crowded in, demanding and cheating; Boers and Britons were equally insistent. The descendants and successors of these white invaders still own two thirds of the agricultural land of the Swazi people.

Nor were the gathered Nguni groups always quiet and orderly. But whenever Moshweshwe had a rebel within his own borders, it was found that this rebel had outside support, sometimes from a mission, other than the Paris Evangelical, which was his mission and which had considerable influence with his people, though the version of Christianity which emerged was distinctly Basutoised. The king must have watched with interest the hatreds between the missions, all supposed to be preaching love.

Sometimes Moshweshwe had to assert himself against both rebels and missions. But at the same time he wanted peace, to see good crops and grazing cattle. War with Europeans was no longer a splendid matter of young warriors wetting their spears. Far too many people got killed in it without even having had the joy of combat first. Better keep out of it, even at the cost of giving up a piece of land or a herd of cattle.

By 1852 the Transvaal and the Free States had come into being, with rudimentary constitutions. But they seemed good enough to poor and almost illiterate people, cut off from the world where modern thought was taking place. Every Boer farmer was also a fighter, marrying young and producing a large family. They feuded with one another when there was no-one else to fight, reading the bits of the Old Testament which suited them. In fact they were typical frontiersfolk. It looked at this point as though, as far as the whites were concerned, southern Africa might be made into a series of small and vulnerable states, compared with which Moshweshwe of the Mountain had considerable power.

After the *Mfecane* was over, there were remains of groups and chiefdoms everywhere, many of whom wanted to go back to the old lands. One begins to see recognisable tribal names more or less on the land where they are now, five generations later. But many of the great fighting tribes of those days are now a handful of depressed and stubborn people, shut into reserves which are too dry and small for the cattle they dream about, while their grandfathers' grazing grounds are now modernish farms, usually owned by white settlers. The young men grumble and brood or else go off to the towns and the break-up of moral order there which may in the end be more disastrous than ever the *Mfecane* was.

If a tribe came back to its old lands and found, as it often did, that the land had been taken over by white farmers and that these white farmers refused to give leave for grazing, claiming that they 'owned' the land, all those miles and miles of it, then there might be trouble. The British Government began tentatively to establish reserves where whites—other than missions—were not supposed to claim land or other privileges, and also to take seriously native law and custom. For the Boers, and no doubt for most British settlers as well, this was nonsense. Nor were the missionaries always pleased, for they wanted to see their own version of Bible law and custom. Yet at least the administrators usually meant well; they did not, like the farmers, think that an African was almost automatically an enemy, something to be destroyed, though in another sense he was part of a cheap labour force.

It was a situation full of fear and resentment. The young Boer Republics were poor; they could not afford a civil service or indeed any other public service except their church. They knew there were minerals on some of their land, but did not work them, preferring to remain as farmers.

The one solid factor always to be reckoned with in southern Africa was Moshweshwe on his mountain, Moshweshwe the diplomat with his alliances, his friendships, his occasional threats and his certainty that sooner or later there would be war between the Basuto and the Boers of the Republics. He tried to put off the evil days as long as he could, meanwhile collecting horses, the war beasts, arms, some home-made cannon, and training an army. But age was creeping up on him and already his sons were quarrelling and taking up positions for the day which would come. We shall see what happened.

There were other wars. The western Xhosa did not take easily 1819 to white rule. The prophet Makana rallied the warriors, helping them to overcome the terror of the new weapons. After him came other wars under the leadership of Hintsa. We name among the heroes the Chiefs Sandele and Krele and Adam Kok, all trying 1834 to keep their African identity and independence, though in different ways. Perhaps we should also name another Xhosa hero, Tiyo Soga, ordained minister of the Church of Scotland, caught between loyalty to his Chief and his mission.

Then came the terrible January of 1856, when the Xhosa and Tembu in the south saw visions and listened to prophecies of an appointed day when signs would appear in the sky, a whirlwind would sweep away the white men to wherever they had come from, and the dead heroes would rise, followed by cattle and corn and a golden age. To achieve this no crops must be planted and all fat cattle killed. The prophetess, Nongqauze, following in the footsteps of Makana was, like Joan of Arc before her, a young girl, but this time a princess. She was believed.

But the day came and the whites were not removed by any whirlwind. There were no signs in the sky, only on earth the sign of starvation, of death coming to thousands, perhaps millions of people. The British Administration under Sir George Grey, which had watched with some horror, sent food, and of course troops. It could have been 'a native rising'. But starving people do not rise. The dead African heroes had not come back to them. Not yet.

Eleven

Missionaries and Explorers

Fertile Egypt was too desirable a prize to be let alone. The Mamelukes, originally slave soldiers, had taken over as rulers under remote control from Istanbul and the Egyptian people had to bear the intolerably costly burden of their pride and quarrels. Napoleon came and went. Then an Albanian Turk, Muhammad Ali, who started life as a tough young soldier, was able to free the country from some of its many masters, who were pulling it to pieces; though he governed with an iron hand he was welcomed and respected and ended as Pasha of Egypt. 1805–1849

Muhammad Ali murdered five hundred Mameluke emirs whose host he had been, but perhaps there was no other way to stability and national prosperity. His programme of public works, including education, irrigation and the introduction of long staple cotton, did much for Egypt. Although the country was still nominally part of the crumbling Ottoman Empire, he was its actual ruler. He extended his domains, revived trade—and with it the pilgrimages—and rationalised the slave trade, using the Sudan as his base for annual slave and ivory campaigns. The old sultanate of Funj came to an end. All went swimmingly for him until he got in the way of the European powers in the Mediterranean, and suffered his first reverse at Navarino. He realised 1827 that he must have, and pay for, European—usually French—arms and technicians. In order to pay for this he had to put through important economic reforms, with new cash crops. He also found it necessary to educate young Egyptians, with the usual result of education—the beginning of a nationalist movement.

But later Khedives were neither as capable nor as ruthless. They began to get worried about the slave trade, even to listen to its opponents. By now the slave recruits to the Egyptian army had been largely replaced. A European technical adviser, able to aim and also to look after a battery of cannon, was worth a lot of slave soldiers with swords. Other kinds of trade looked more **1863–1879** profitable. The Khedive Ismail's imagination was increasingly attracted by steamships and railways. In fact, one of the world's earliest railways ran from Alexandria to Cairo.

In East Africa, however, the slave trade, growing every century increasingly disastrous for the inland victims, was too profitable for any ruler to give up. By the mid-nineteenth century the chaos of warring cities and rulers along the coast was beginning **1806–1856** to take shape as a trading empire under Seyyid Majid Ibn Said, whose headquarters were in Zanzibar. Here and on the coast, Arab traders, Indian businessmen and, increasingly, some Africans or part-Africans, lived in comfort and growing luxury. It was Seyyid Said who built up the commercial contacts which his father had begun; by 1859 the total trade of Zanzibar was £1½ million. Over £55,000 of this was in cloves, first planted here in 1818. Already perhaps, Zanzibar smelt as it does now, so that when one first lands a warm breath meets one from cloves, cinnamon, drying coconuts and the marvellous fruit markets where all that is most delicious, most highly coloured and dripping with scented juice, is piled in baskets; golden mangoes bursting with their own weight, scarlet lychees and every lesser fruit from Asia or Africa.

But in those days the slave market, where now a grey and rather forbidding cathedral towers, was packed with slaves, probably not for sale to France or Portugal or even America, but certainly to the Indies and locally to rulers or merchants. It was only when something as bad as a cholera epidemic broke out that the price of slaves dropped.

The first mission to Zanzibar went out in 1844, and was received in a friendly way. Others followed. But it was a difficult environment. All missions believed that slavery was wrong, and that runaways must be helped. Yet how to do this without violating the laws of private property? This made for strain.

Yet Islam also had its standards. It was in 1848 that the all-powerful Kabaka Suna of Uganda was accused by an Arab from Zanzibar, probably a trader shocked by the casual killing that went on in his court: 'Thou and those whom thou killest have been created alike by Allah. To Allah alone thou owest thy throne and it is a grievous sin before Allah to destroy those whom he hath created.' Suna was apparently interested in this curious doctrine but not converted.

It is doubtful whether there was much intention of making converts to Islam amongst the ordinary inland Africans. After all, a professing Moslem could not be enslaved and this might be inhibiting. But probably Islam and the possession of *Ustaralu*, that is Arab Swahili culture, was one of the main factors for the breakdown of the tribal structure in eastern Africa. The pull to the towns meant that there was an easy religious and social change-over. On the west African coast you were more likely to bring your tribal feelings and relationships along with you to Lome, Accra, Abidjan or Conakry, just as you would to the new mining cities in central and southern Africa.

The trade routes inland from Zanzibar or from the coastal town of Bagamoyo were also the routes for explorers and missionaries. In all the missionary narratives one comes on 'the horrors of the slave trade', fully as bad as anything on the west coast had been. The later journeys of Livingstone started from the east coast, though his earlier ones started from the Cape.

How should we, nowadays, assess Livingstone, this spiritually 1813-1873 ruthless and singlehearted man? He was a medical missionary, trained in Glasgow. He was always certain that he was right. Nor did he question what came after him, trade, order and peace, and an industrious life for those who had been idle: the ending of much of African life, not only features which he deplored, such as nakedness, tribal warfare and polygamy, but much which had a definite social purpose which he did not see or would not have been willing to understand. He did not believe in the superiority of whites, only that he himself knew best, something rather different. Better surely that many of the Batswana got their first sight of the white world from missionaries who at least had certain ideals and who were not there to exploit and enslave them, than from the Trekkers for whom they were enemies. For the best of the missionaries no human soul was an enemy; they tried to understand; they made friends. They and their wives gave much practical help. For them the enemy to be wrestled with was the whole continent, so full of dangers and horrors and the darkness of the unknown.

Exploration was something which excited people in Europe, just as space travel does now. And there was beauty to be described for the first time in English, as Livingstone did for the Victoria Falls: 'Scenes so lovely must have been gazed upon by angels in their flight'. But there were also scenes of horror which led him to work out 'a policy for Africa' designed first to save the African people, whom he seems to have liked more than he did many of his own white colleagues, from the Portuguese in Angola. Livingstone was over fifty when he started his last journey from Zanzibar, saying 'I shall enjoy myself and feel that I am doing my duty'.

1855 Speke, Grant, Stanley and Baker were not missionaries but purely explorers, though Stanley was the first modern in the sense that he was writing consciously for publication, starting in 1866 as correspondent for the *Missouri Democrat*. He was no woolly-minded idealist, but kept his own career firmly in mind, even when it meant shutting his eyes to atrocities by his employers. (see Chapter 12). The explorers always took Western values with them, and were as convinced as the missionaries that they had the right answers. It must have seemed so in the Europe which was surging forward, ever more and more prosperous, in spite of occasional wars which did not however affect fashionable or intellectual life. I mention only a few of the explorers from various European countries. Baikie was an Orkneyman, who in 1854 went out in a tiny steamer and canoed up the Niger; and Benue was an explorer and scientist, with the warm curiosity of a Darwin, he was the first commander not to lose a single man by fever, but he saw to it that they took their quinine. Baines was a surveyor by profession, an artist by aptitude. Burton (1821-1899) was a dramatiser of himself and his acutely observed surroundings. Yet how could any of those African travellers avoid this dramatisation? All of them behaved with immense courage, and this is perhaps truest of all for the golden-haired Mrs. Baker, who between 1862 and 1894 went everywhere with her husband.

For most Africans such people as these must have been the first Europeans they saw. But they seldom recorded their impressions, except for instance, in the unflattering but obviously interested sculpture of the west coast. We know that Stanley tried to convert the Kabaka Mutesa, but Mutesa did not think in at all the same way; for him religion was politics, and these strange religions were a direct challenge to himself-as-god. Certainly if one is God, or if one is within a culture where god-kings are taken seriously, other religions cannot be lightly accepted.

In fact the next Ugandan Kabaka, Mwanga, began to feel shaken about being a god-king. In this situation, to lose confidence for a moment is to lose everything. For other people lose confidence too : those who have for centuries accepted the necessity for sacrifice, who have paid in their lives as easily as you pay a cheque into a bank. Then the relationship between Kabaka and people breaks; he is no longer so essential to them that all he demands must be done.

In this situation many people in Uganda, among them the most intelligent and sensitive, became Christians and felt immense satisfaction in this new focusing of life. Those who became Christians or Moslems—for there were many Moslem converts—must have felt as though they were just waking from a dream, a formal nightmare. No wonder they were ready for martyrdom. A little later there was intense and bloody rivalry between Protestants 1885 and Catholics. In 1897 an infant Kabaka was baptised and brought up under a Christian regency. The Kabakaship was deliberately westernised. And yet perhaps even now a mystique remains. There is of course a royal mystique in Great Britain, but it is not extended to the family nowadays, as it was until lately extended in Uganda to the Queen-mother and Queen-sister. In Uganda again, the Katikiro was more than just a Prime Minister. Well, Presidents and Prime Ministers are built up in other countries in other ways; readers of newspapers still feel that they are in some way 'different'.

After the missionaries came the traders. People who went in for trade had much to gain, all over Africa, from this opening up, which cut out some of the cost to the coast; they had a far greater variety of trade goods and if the traders dealt honestly by them, good friendships were made. But there was also this business of peace and security. Tribes which had gone in for raiding, and those with wide grazing lands, were more likely to be unfriendly. Peace restricted them. And again, a well-armed

European caravan was likely to shoot at sight. This seems to have been specially true of the Germans.

The Khedives of Egypt were on the look-out for administrators; in this way the explorer, Baker, became Governor of the Sudan. He had plenty of power but found it harder to be one of the Khedive Ismail's administrators than it had been to journey up the Nile. Egypt would have liked to push out its frontiers towards the south, but communications were too difficult. General 1874 Gordon followed him as Governor, and then as we shall see came the revolution by the Mahdi and the end of Egyptian rule in the Sudan. (See Chapter 16.)

Meanwhile, an independent robber lord, the same kind of man as the founders of many European noble families, took over power in Ethiopia. His name was Ras Kassa but he was crowned as the Emperor Theodore, and he it was who brought modern arms and army organisation into that ancient kingdom of his. He was an extremely intelligent man, but unhappily he did not see far enough to avoid ill-treating two peaceable British envoys, and this was followed by the first British punitive expedition, when in 1867 the fortress of Magdala was taken and the Emperor of Ethiopia shot himself. (See Chapter 16.)

And in the south? The last whirlpools of the *Mfecane* were still circling. Some of the peoples, Nguni and others, who had felt Shaka's hand heavy on them and had refused to come into his empire, started north. Part of the Nguni crossed the Zambezi about 1835, marched quickly north, and only settled for a time after they had got to the southern end of Lake Tanganyika. They had started as a march of young Ngoni warriors, but took on the men from the tribes they had defeated on the way, no doubt gathering themselves wives as well. This in turn set up a movement of population. People fled from them, their chiefs were killed, their social order broke down, and they ended by joining with the Ngoni, separate now from the main Nguni, or themselves set off on plundering expeditions.

On the whole the Ngoni regiments, under the *indunas*, kept themselves together, and, when one *induna* went off in one direction and another in another, they probably did not fight until a generation or more had gone by. If they set up something like a state, they tended to be a ruling class, though it was not always the old Ngoni language which in the end came to be the one that most people used.

When one gets a close-up look at them again, in the early 20th century, there were still conquest traditions; people preferred to think of themselves as descendants of the winners. Some of John Chilembwe's followers (see Chapter 14) may have had grand-fathers among the *indunas*. For by that time they were mostly settled in what came to be known as Nyasaland and is now Malawi. There is a splendid Easter hymn in Citumbuka set to the war song of the chief northern Ngoni *induna*.

One must, I think, remember that Christianity is a potentially explosive religion, at any rate if one takes the New Testament seriously, and does not make for submissiveness in human rela-tions. It started as a religion of the oppressed and says things like 'He has filled the hungry with good things and the rich He hath sent empty away'. If people are genuinely hungry they will be more than likely to take this at its simplest meaning. And if those who have taught them appear not to take it seriously, then the congregations will quite possibly go off and devise something which seems to them nearer to the genuine idea of Christianity. And again, all missions believed in education, and education is explosive too. People who are educated will not put up with being treated as though they are dirt. And a Christian education lays stress on the value of the individual whereas those who are looking for cheap labour cannot afford to think of people as in-dividuals. For them the 'mission-trained native' who wore Euro-pean clothes and did not take off his hat automatically to any white, was always to be blamed for any act of rebellion, any attempt to alter the white domination, upheld by the power of money and guns.

It must have seemed odd to many of the Africans amongst whom the missionaries worked, who were people with consider-able intelligence and watchfulness in human relationships, to see the quarrels that went on. But it was certainly a way of diverting the angry whites against one another, and to some extent, pro-tecting themselves. The nature and methods of propitiation of the new God varied from mission to mission, though some of the basic stories were the same, and were acceptable, especially as many of them embodied values which were known already in

other stories and myths. One thing which all Christian (but not
Moslem) missions agreed on was monogamy. Now, monogamy
fits in very well with the Western theory of romantic love, and
with the beginnings of nineteenth century feminism, though it
does not really work unless birth control is widely known about
and practised. Its enforcement caused immense suffering,
especially to the wives who were cast off, for no fault of their
own, with nobody to protect them or look after their children.
It also placed a heavy burden on the remaining wife. Naturally
people got round it in various ways, as indeed they do in Europe
and America. But the missionaries could only think of marriage
in terms of their own culture.

The clash between two concepts of Christianity was very clear
in South Africa. The London Missionary Society, working mostly
north from Kuruman, along the 'Missionary Road', was constantly up against the Boers, whose version could never include
friendships with natives, the 'children of Ham', just as the Portuguese version, current in Angola, did not encourage thoughts of
1849 humanity with 'the animals', their black slaves. Robert Moffat,
Livingstone's father-in-law, was the main Church Missionary
Society influence during half a century; like so many missionaries, he was a lowland Scot, not very well-educated, though with
many interests; he was of course untouched by the idea that
other cultures had moral value. He was on terms of real friendship with Mzilikazi, though he never converted him. He did,
however, convert the young Khama, Chief of the Bamangwato
(see Chapter 15). It was Mzilikazi who said 'The Bamangwato
are dogs, but Khama is a man'. If Moffat had been unhampered
by political pressures, could he have made peace there? He did at
least learn the language thoroughly, did much translation and
brought in what ideas of public health were available in his time.
Above all he was not out for personal gain, did not lie and was
very brave. Such qualities count.

Twelve

The Scramble

I start this chapter with a map showing what an imaginative and intelligent man, the young Harry Johnston, wanted to do with Africa. As I have already suggested, the mid-Victorian British were so occupied with their own traditional interests that only a few thought about Africa and then rather as something with which to play European power politics. But they did it with the minimum of trouble and expenditure.

The Portuguese still held on to their old slaving territories, though, by the nineties, they were on the verge of insolvency in Mozambique and harassed by Gunguwhana of Gazaland. Most of the Angolans were shipped to the cocoa plantations on São Tomé. Chocolate was becoming an increasingly popular food in, for example, England, and although by the end of the century the slaves were supposed to be willing wage earners, this was not actually the case. From Mozambique they might go to the French sugar plantations on Réunion Island or to Madagascar. In both countries there was domestic slavery, especially of women, with the usual results. While the slave trade went on—in spite of the very genuine anger and concern from some Portuguese statesmen in Europe—it did not appear necessary to those in the colonies to develop other trades or industries. However, at the end of the century when the Rand gold mines started, labour could be exported from Mozambique into South Africa and ingeniously enough most of the wages of that labour could then be collected by the exporting country. The London Foreign Office, anxious for the success of the gold mines, tried not to listen to anti-slavery denunciations. The Portuguese were England's ancient allies.

In the north Anglo-French control of Egypt and the Suez 1881

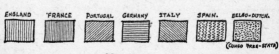

Map 8

Canal went along nicely until Arabi Pasha led the first Egyptian national uprising, making to the Khedive Tewfiq the classic statement: 'We are not your slaves and we shall not be bought from this day on.' This ended in British rule over Egypt but at the price of giving Germany a free hand elsewhere in Africa. The German exploring and trading companies who followed the German missionaries in east Africa went through the usual process of 'buying' land from alleged chiefs who fingerprinted 'treaties'; soon afterwards came the calling in of soldiers to put down 'risings'. In 1885 Carl Peters got himself and the German Colonisation Society a remarkable charter from his own government, forbidding nothing, enjoining nothing, not even making the usual European excuse that slavery was to be put down. In this spirit and backed by Bismarck, German power was established on the east coast of Africa. Villages were burnt and the inhabitants flogged and murdered. Peter's Society was interested in the settlement of German peasants; they would need safe and empty land. When Peters was recalled to Germany there was some official condemnation but later he was reinstated.

The missions, especially perhaps those of the Benedictines, did their best in a bad situation. They educated up to a point and taught some industrial and agricultural skills. But the great Christian voice of protest is not to be found. Still less does it come from the Portuguese possessions. Bismarck was also backing German annexations elsewhere in Africa, in the Cameroons, now trebly divided between European powers, in Togoland and, most importantly, in south-west Africa. But all was done, less from an interest in having African possessions than from his intentions in Europe. The Germans, now politically unified, wanted 'a place in the sun'. Bismarck saw to it.

In west Africa the French were gradually extending what was coming to be a colonial empire, further and further inland. This kind of expansion often came as a result of local initiative rather than that of the government in Europe. By 1893 the French colonies in west Africa had definitely taken shape. Although the Ivory Coast, French Guinea, and, slightly later, Dahomey, were officially established with boundaries and administrations, French penetration inland along the Senegal river and its upper tributaries had also gone ahead. But it was not an easy conquest. One of Uthman dan Fodio's aristocratic followers had made the pilgrimage to Mecca. He came back, now as Al Haj Umar, married one of dan Fodio's daughters and methodically began to prepare an army which would destroy the infidel kingdoms between the Senegal and the western Niger. It was his son, Ahmadu, whom the French met in their advance from the mouth of the Senegal, but it took many years before the loosely strung empire fell to pieces after defeated Ahmadu had his head cut off by pagans 1898 whom he had tried to conquer. Then Samori, the Mandingo leader, also a Moslem, put up a strong resistance among the southern Mande people, who remember him as a hero, before in the end he too was defeated.

That was the signal for the French to go ahead. They had by now met the British on the upper Niger. Bornu was in decline, barely keeping a kind of independence beyond the large empire of the Fulani of Hausaland whose states, each based on a handsome, thriving city and with a certain degree of technical and scientific knowledge and efficient administration, held together in alliances. Their wars of conquest and slave raiding were against the infidels on their borders. But British trade penetration and treaties with leading rulers led finally to a situation of colonial rule, especially when the British wanted to keep out the French. It had to be the British flag that was flown next to that of the sultan or emir who usually continued, subject to certain restrictions, to administer his old territories.

However, spheres of influence were more or less amicably worked out between the European powers. It did not matter whether or not their boundaries were or were not the natural ethnic or language boundaries of the 'natives', unless there was a specially powerful ruler who was worth placating. What mattered was the protection of French or British traders against one another's competition. Sierra Leone and Liberia started in the early nineteenth century as settlements for freed slaves both from the plantations and from ships. These ex-slaves came from various west African countries and language groups and were mostly Christian converts, all the more enthusiastic and sincere since they had so obviously been deserted by their own gods and rescued by the followers of the Christian God. With Christianity they tended to take on the current nineteenth century Christian ideas about thrift, industry and enterprise. Nationalism here, when it came, took on a correspondingly different tone.

We must remember that up to the last quarter of the nineteenth century the colonial powers did everything as cheaply as possible; for this reason they preferred to leave as much as possible to trading companies : the risk, the shame and the profits. The scramble for Africa, though there were heroic episodes, was often ignoble and accidental. By the last third of the century Great Britain was left with a number of undeveloped territories especially on the west coast, left over from slaving and gold-trading days. Few people were interested in them. The natives were scarcely people at all. But the lives of the European soldiers and petty traders were hardly considered more valuable.

Lives were cheap in Europe too. One need go no further than the Crimean War to see massive disregard for the lives and miseries of the ordinary English soldier. The 'working classes' in all the European countries which were now going ahead so splendidly with the Industrial Revolution and further enrichment of the newly rich, were considered just as different in kind by most of the ruling classes as Africans were by the whites. There were of course exceptions among the ruling and almost ruling classes, especially in the radical church, most of all perhaps in England; they were called philanthropists. This word comes from the Greek and means 'lovers of mankind'; this was considered rather an odd, off-beat thing to be; perhaps it still is.

Meanwhile there was another pair of eyes on Africa with a very good brain when its own narrow money and power interests were at stake—King Leopold of the Belgians. He did nothing so 1835-1909 crude as national conquest; instead he established a chain of scientific and trading stations across Africa; the cover name was the African International Association. Philanthropy was much mentioned. The explorer and writer Stanley was his highly reputable-seeming agent.

Before settling on Africa King Leopold had glanced round the world, giving some thought to south-eastern Asia and its possible exploitation. But Africa and finally the Congo area seemed most suitable and the rubber trade the most obviously modern and lucrative. The methods which were used for getting the full quota of rubber out of the inhabitants, including the cutting off of right

hands, were so horrible and in time, owing to the unpopular
1903 revelations of Casement and Morel, became so notorious, that
he had to hand over his private empire to the Belgian Government. This meant a less harsh rule although there were still bad
patches. One cannot reform local methods or ways of thinking
overnight.

What must be emphasised here is that Leopold's empire went
far beyond the bounds of the original country of the Bakongo.
Anything likely to be profitable was seized upon. As soon as his
agents discovered copper, diamonds or whatever it might be, the
boundaries were moved. In this way adjoining countries such
as the very rich Katanga were included. Its able king, M'Siri,
keen on trade but averse to slave traders on either side, was
attacked by King Leopold's soldiers and was unable to get
through in time to Cecil Rhodes, from whom he might have got
slightly better terms. What is called Congo is really a number of
different countries, some with very valuable raw materials, some
without; they have different standards, different languages and
customs. Bakongo, Baluba, Lulua, Luvale, Kwango, Kile and
others are organised tribally, though this usually takes the form of
rival political parties with rival leaders. Congo is not yet a nation
though if the various peoples within its borders really choose to
come together without outside interference for their mutual
advantage and comfort, it may be. They have the advantage of a
martyr figure, Patrice Lumumba. But the present boundaries are
among the most unreal that exist, even in Africa, casually cutting
across families and clans, grabbing or excluding small nations or
parts of nations. If they had been deliberately designed to encourage civil war they could scarcely have been worse. The Baluba
are of course the Luba people already mentioned in Chapter 8,
many of whom are in Zambia; the boundary between Congo-
Kinshasa and Zambia is simply part of a fairly recent carve-up
by European (and American) mining interests.

It was Leopold's Congo grab that was beginning in the nineteenth century to alert the other European powers, though Portuguese slave trading and settling went on steadily on both coasts.
Earlier, Livingstone had said 'I direct your attention to Africa'.
But until it seemed really profitable European countries were unwilling to be directed, except perhaps to South Africa where

the Cape paradise, so beautiful and healthy, had attracted settlers.

The general course of colonial occupation in South Africa was firstly, a settlement along the edges, not only in Cape Colony, with its fine towns and country houses and general air of civilisation, but wherever there was a good harbour and fertile hinterland, as with the German settlements at Walvis Bay. The British always seemed to import an organisation of government, civil, military and religious, with a class system developing as soon as might be. They had money, some of which they spent on pleasing architecture, schools and 'charities' and they despised those without these amenities, whether black or white. But the Boer Trekkers went north up the middle of the country, forming themselves into small, classless and somewhat unorganised states wherever they found land which they could occupy, hoping to avoid tsetse fly belts, and with their rifles always at the ready. Natal was for a time a Boer republic under Pretorius following the defeat of King Dingane (Chapter 10), but was annexed by Britain in 1845, after which most of the Boer settlers moved away again, to be replaced by assisted British emigrants. A land Commission by now had allocated some two million acres out of the twelve-and-a-half million of Natal to the 'natives', but these were not the best lands. The British, especially those who wanted to live fairly peaceably, without too much expenditure on military expeditions, were in a continual state of distrust of the expanding Boers and uncertain whom they could deal with.

The British colonies tended to cluster round the appurtenances of government. With the Boers, getting together was not thought of in terms of a city, but of a *laager,* an armed camp, or an equally militant prayer meeting : otherwise, freedom and the wide spaces. It was difficult even for them to get people to attend the Volksraad meetings or to agree on a written constitution, still less to get any taxes paid. Neither concept of colonisation took any notice of 'natives' except as servants or possible enemies, to be contained by treaties or force.

After the Zulu wars of conquest had died down, the various displaced groups and tribes began to come back into their old lands, sometimes with their old leaders, sometimes with a younger generation. But all too often they found that this land, some of which had been virtually emptied by Shaka's policy of having a 'scorched earth' belt between him and the whites, was now divided up between Boer farmers. Small groups might simply become farm workers, hungry and conquered. But some of the larger tribes, realising that it was to be war, built themselves hill forts. The Pedi kingdom in the eastern Transvaal was established in the Lulu mountains. The Tlokwa, the Ngawane, the Hlubi and others, all dispossessed during the *Mfecane,* made themselves into organised bodies of raiders, attacking other Sotho or Nguni groups wherever they saw an opening. But later under Queen Mantathisi the Batlokwa moved into two mountain strongholds north of the Caledon river and for a time ruled the surrounding country.

But there was no unity. Tsonga fought with Tsonga, Tswana with Tswana. There was seldom a chief strong enough to impose his rule on others, apart from Moshweshwe himself. The Boers did their best to stop the Africans getting guns or ammunition, going so far as to sack David Livingstone's house, since he was known to have supplied arms for defence to Kgosi Sechele of the Bakwena as well as being bitterly critical of Boer attitudes. The Transvaal burghers pressed constantly on the settled people, wherever there was good land. Adam Kok found himself forced to lead his Griquas, who had already been forced far from their homeland in the Cape, in a trek out of the fertile belt along the Caledon and across the Drakensberg to what became known as East Griqualand. Here they were let alone for a time until diamonds began to be found in their fields.

In the course of a century there were nine 'Kaffir Wars'. We are carefully told how many Europeans were killed in each, and of their undoubted heroism, but we are never told how many were killed on the other side. That was not thought of as the material of history. The 'Kaffirs' rebelled; of course they had to be killed; that was that. It is up to us now to look with greater care. The leaders in these wars are only worth a footnote as rebels in most history books, but their names and words still live, not least in the great speech by Nelson Mandela, President of the African National Congress, a man who hated bloodshed, but had to lead Umkonto we Sizwe into violence and sabotage when nothing else availed. His words at the Rivonia treason trial in a sense echo those of Makana five generations before him : 'People say I made this war. Let me see whether my delivering myself up to the conquerors will restore peace to my country.'

But while the fighting was still going on, between 1884 and 1886 the South African gold fields were opened up. The first diamonds were discovered in 1867 and in another year or two they were being taken seriously. Unfortunately perhaps, they still are, not only for decoration but for industry. Other minerals were discovered or suspected, and the British South Africa Company was founded in 1888.

But first the Zulus had to be dealt with. We must go back to the death of King Dingane of the ama-Zulu and the succession of his brother Mpande in 1840 (Chapter 10). Mpande was on the whole a peaceable man, well aware of the danger of the situation of the Zulu nation between the Boers of the Transvaal on the north west and the Swazi, hereditary enemies but not to be feared in the same way. Between the Zulu country and the sea was the British colony of Natal, also exerting pressure, though in a less aggressive way than the Boers. King Mpande had a fifteen year old son called Cetshwayo who was getting his military training in the old Zulu way under strict discipline, marching or running, always barefoot in Shaka's tradition, learning every trick of shield and assegai and also, of course, learning about the history and traditions of the ama-Zulu and the the administration of Zulu justice. No doubt, being an intelligent boy, he also thought about the new weapons of war, the Tower muskets and the newer rifles and even cannon, and also about horses. The new weapons were gradually modifying the older Zulu battle tactics. Most African nations had by now taken to horses to some extent but not so far as to organise cavalry, still less to use horses or mules for transport.

There was constant pressure on the Zulus from Boer raiders seizing their cattle, their women and children, claiming land on the strength of invented concessions. Theophilus Shepstone, whom the Zulus called 'Somtseu', Secretary for Native Affairs in Natal and much liked and trusted, was considerably worried about the affairs of Zululand, partly because of the misbehaviour of the Transvaalers, partly because of the violence of the young Cetshwayo who killed his rival and half-brother in the fearful slaughter of Ndondakusaka. What was he going to be like?

Yet on Mpande's death the Zulu council asked Somtseu, 'Father to the king's children' to go into Zululand and crown the prince. This he did in spite of efforts from the President of the Transvaal to intervene, and was everywhere well received. It was felt that this was an omen of peace and indeed it seems that the goodwill of Natal was real and that Shepstone himself had a very genuine understanding of the Zulu people. Because Europe itself was becoming a little more humane Shepstone hoped that the Zulus would do the same. He hoped for less punishment by death, better trials and in general a way of life which would commend itself to the ways of thought of the philanthropists, though he knew that 'It cannot be expected that the amelioration described will immediately take effect'. The Zulu council also asked Shepstone to try and settle all outstanding quarrels with the Boers lest war should come. The last thing they wanted was a war with the whites.

Yet Cetshwayo's warriors were restless. They wanted to fight the Swazi people and were angry when the Natal government stopped them. Nor was King Cetshwayo pleased when the same government intervened in a domestic matter, punishment of some men and young women who had acted in defiance of him. Anyone brought up in the European tradition would have been bound to sympathise with the lovers who had been punished by death, but it was tactlessly handled and Cetshwayo reacted by saying: 'Did I ever tell Mr. Shepstone I would not kill? . . . I do kill: but do not consider that I have done anything yet in the way of killing. Why do white people start at nothing? I have not yet begun; I have yet to kill, it is the custom of our nation and I shall not depart from it. Why does the Governor of Natal speak to me about our laws? Do I go to Natal and dictate to him about his laws? I shall not agree to any laws or rules from Natal and by doing so throw the large *kraal* which I govern into the waters. My people will not listen unless they are killed and while wishing to be friends with the English I do not agree to give my people over to be governed by laws sent to me by them.'

It did not help at all that Cetshwayo had adopted, as his English adviser, the trader and adventurer called Dunn. This man made his way, first, into King Mpande's confidence, then into his son's. The Africans had still much to learn about the motives and promises of the whites. A few old muskets, sold to Cetshwayo at a huge profit, brought Dunn a large grant of land, wives and cattle, and powers equivalent to those of a chief. Cetshwayo loved Dunn as a brother, but from the first Dunn was out for his own advantage. The brotherhood was all on one side.

Meanwhile, how was it at Thaba Bosiu, the Mountain of the Night, where the country which is now Lesotho was coming into being? During the '60s, not only Zululand, but the whole of southern Africa was in turmoil, as the Voortrekkers became more confident, richer, able to buy better arms, ambitious for power, certain that they were the chosen people, angry with the British officials who tried to contain them and their ardours. The Boers were constantly seizing more land and the various chiefdoms were constantly hitting back, or moving off with their cattle, but probably leaving rear guards behind to plough a quick crop and harass the newcomers. Everyone stole oxen from everyone else. There was always a reason for a small war.

And then came a more serious attack on the Basotho. This time King Moshweshwe, now an old man, had a serious opponent in the Boer leader, Jan Hendrik Brand. Both sides were well armed; after initial wins by the Basotho, badly followed up because of jealousy and short-sightedness, the Free Staters moved in and besieged Thaba Bosiu. But Moshweshwe had a new way out; he declared that he had given his country to the Queen— hence the Protectorate status. Brand's aim was to break up Lesotho and drive the tribes in all directions, but the British thought otherwise, though they still made things fairly difficult for Moshweshwe. He died in 1870, with his boundaries shrunken, the Boers having managed to take much of the best agricultural land, but at least leaving a nation.

Wars went on. By 1877 there was increasing tension between the Boers and the Zulu people. Inevitably it would lead to large scale war. There were those among the British in Natal who thought that Shepstone should stand back and allow Boers and Zulu to destroy one another. Yet perhaps Shepstone was wise to try and avoid it, not only for the sake of the ama-Zulu, his friends, but also because he could foresee that it might mean total war

between black and white, the thing that everyone dreaded. In-
1878 stead came the official annexation of the Transvaal. Britain took
over the whole responsibility of the country. This meant putting
its financial affairs into order, with the continual payments of
regular salaries to officials. It also meant that the British Government took over an old quarrel between the Zulu and Boers about
the boundary line. There were several attempts at arbitration.
Perhaps if Shepstone had been left alone it might have been possible to come to some peaceable solution.

But he was not. The new British High Commissioner, Sir
Bartle Frere, had come out in 1877. He seems to have been determined almost from the beginning on the conquest of the Zulu
nation and he had already had considerable experience of this
kind of thing in India. If this was to be done the Zulu had to
be made to appear as a menace to the British government and
the electors of Great Britain. Here we will let Frances Colenso
speak: she is writing back to England to people who were being
subjected to anti-African propaganda the whole time. The Zulu
—and other Africans—themselves could not have said what was
happening. They had not realised the power of propaganda. But
Bishop Colenso of Natal, the heretic and friend of the ama-Zulu,
was a social anthropologist ahead of his time. He and his family
understood and struggled to undo some of the evil which was
being done. His wife writes: 'You may (if you will) just disbelieve
all histories of Zulu cruelty which are industriously invented and
circulated by those who wish to back up the government in this
way by exciting a feeling of hatred for the Zulu.' And again,
later: 'I declare I am ashamed to look black people in the face.'

There was a commission of enquiry set up. Forgeries on the
Boer side circulated freely. They were believed or alleged to be
believed; the Zulus were not believed. Nor was King Cetshwayo
or the Zulu council informed of the findings of the commission.
One unfortunate incident after another took place; Cetshwayo
held his people back for as long as he could, organising hunts
instead of war. Like other southern African kings he was not an
absolute ruler; he was bound to take the advice of his council.
And Frere was determined on war: Frances Colenso speaks of
'the persevering attempts to irritate the Zulu King, to malign
him, etc.'. He sent an ultimatum to Cetshwayo of a kind which

no independent or even semi-independent ruler could be expected to comply with and giving a time limit which was almost impossible. Those who know Scottish history may remember that other time limit set on Macdonald of Glencoe, which ended with the killing of the Highland 'rebels' by the forces of the Government in circumstances which now seem shameful.

Cetshwayo's men gathered at the king's *kraal* in great heart. But Cetshwayo himself must have known that although he had the numbers, the other side had the weapons, and that these in the end would be decisive. Dunn, the English adviser, tried to dissuade the king from war but when this was impossible deserted with all his own people. On the British side the Commander-in-Chief was the strangely incompetent Lord Chelmsford. When the ultimatum to Cetshwayo had not been complied with in the short time limit, the British invaded Zululand across the Tugela.

In the astonishing mixture of heroism in the lower ranks of officers and enlisted men, combined with monumental stupidity on top, which was characteristic of British armies up to World War I at least, the British army was defeated and almost annihilated at Isandhlwana. This was followed by another semi-defeat 1879 at Rorke's Drift, though here the immense courage of the defenders had made it possible to evacuate patients in the hospital which was attacked. But other British columns went on into Zululand and it must have been clear to King Cetshwayo that this was an all-out attack. All the same he is reported to have said: 'The English are attacking me in my own country and I will defend myself and my country. I will not send my impis to kill them in Natal because I and those who went before me have always been good friends of the English.' He had hoped that negotiations might be opened and that the war could be halted. But Chelmsford was intent on having his revenge. The Zulu people were given no alternative but war.

The war went on with horrible loss of life, but the British were gradually beginning to understand how to fight this kind of war. Modern weapons and technology were beginning to tell. Some of the Zulu army fell away. There were more attempts at negotiation but always the British demanded terms which King Cetshwayo could not honourably comply with. In the end the Zulu army was defeated at Ulundi with enormous slaughter. Cetshwayo himself fled with only a few followers. Then came the chase of the beaten and hiding king, the rewards for his capture unclaimed by his own people. That picture too is known to people in the Scottish Highlands, whose Prince Charles Edward Stuart, was hidden by one family after another and never betrayed to the English troops, even by the poorest Highlander.

Prisoners were of course taken, threatened and lied to. In the 1879 end Cetshwayo was captured, utterly exhausted. He was imprisoned. His country was divided up in a so-called settlement which fell to pieces as soon as the English who had enforced it withdrew. Shepstone was no longer the Secretary for Native affairs in Natal. Nor can one be certain that, in spite of old friendship and trust, King Cetshwayo would have got justice from him. Frances Colenso certainly believed he would not. Shepstone himself believed in 'divide and rule' and the appointment of minor chiefs who could undermine the Zulu royal family and with it, the Zulu nation although the King was nominally reinstated after a period of exile. The renegade John Dunn had the largest lands and was given charge of Cetshwayo's son and brothers whom he treated almost as slaves. Chelmsford had his revenge.

One of the chiefs, Zibebu, who had been supported by the government and had acquired a large share in the dividing up of Zululand rebelled against Cetshwayo. Cetshwayo weakened and anxious, was defeated and a great number of his loyal supporters killed. The royal *kraal* was burnt and the king wounded. There still seems to have been a feeling in Cetshwayo's mind that his old friend Shepstone and the Queen of England, the Great White Lady, would somehow see that justice was done, but early in February 1884 the king died and was buried by his people. His grave is still an honoured and sacred place.

Thirteen

A close look

How did Africa look from Europe? For almost all European statesmen this was a country on a map inhabited by people who could not really be said to exist because they had not appeared in Europe. However, it was a place which could make and unmake military and missionary reputations. I want in this chapter to take a close look at one country, Botswana, which I happen to know; in many ways what happened there was typical. In this chapter I have used the Setswana word *Kgosi*, which is not 'king' in the European sense, but means more than the slightly derogatory translation: 'chief', since it has in it elements of law-giver, intercessor, leader and food-bringer, and yet always and forever, child of the tribe.

It was noticed with annoyance in Great Britain that the Boer Republics were gradually working their way west towards the 'Missionaries' Road' up through Bechuanaland while the Germans were extending their sphere of influence, and increasing their possessions eastwards from the west coast, although Walvis Bay was a British possession annexed to the Cape. In 1884, Bismarck had annexed Damaraland and Namaqualand as 'protectorates'. This became a useful word, implying no real responsibilities, but warning other European powers to keep out. In order to stop Boers and Germans meeting Bechuanaland was annexed by the British as a protectorate. This was followed by the declaration of a British sphere of interest north of Bechuanaland. But who was to run it? There was no real colonial service yet. The simplest thing was to agree gracefully to the demands of a very rich and extremely energetic English settler, Cecil Rhodes, and let the British South Africa Company run it.

Here we must go back to the time when Cetshwayo was a
young man, the time when a few of the Boer leaders in the Transvaal were beginning to suspect that they might become the richest
country in the world. Rhodes was not the first to think in terms
of a British way up the centre of Africa, though essentially it was
a step in the economic and power war between the British
along the coast and the Boer republics in the central districts of south Africa. But Rhodes and his colleagues, seeing the
poorest of the Boer states, the Transvaal, growing rich almost
overnight from the new gold of the Witwatersrand, was thinking
in terms of other possible goldfields. What might there not be
further north?

It is not easy to make a historical judgement on Cecil Rhodes.
He had a vision of a British Empire which now seems utterly
wrong and yet it was no selfish or merely arrogant and greedy
vision. It was a kind of worship which demanded sacrifice and
he never hesitated to make it, whatever it involved for himself.
For this vision he killed, lied and cheated and wore himself out.
He allowed his gold-seeking followers to destroy priceless historical
evidence. Other kinds of value or truth did not matter to him.
Nor did individual human lives, including perhaps his own.

Before we take our minds from the Boers and their doings to
consider Rhodes, I would like to look in detail at one incident
showing the ordinary treatment of 'natives'. It is no worse than
many others. In the 1870s the Kgatla people were living somewhat west of what is now Pretoria. It was good, well-watered
country where they could graze many cattle and raise crops without destroying the fertility of the land. Their capital was Moru-
leng, the place of the great morula tree. There had been wars
but now they were living peaceably under their chief, Kgamanyane, great-grandfather of my own chief and adopted son, Kgosi
Linchwe II. The Boers came trickling in under their leader, Paul
Kruger. He asked for land and 'apprentices' as they were called.
Kgosi Kgamanyane supposed that he wanted the use of land for
a crop and even helped him, sending his own initiation group
to help the white chief with his ploughing. He did not understand at first that the 'apprentices' were virtually slaves, that they
would be taught the Bible (or rather the Old Testament) and the
whip, overworked and underfed. At first perhaps he did not

bother. Life was pleasant enough; he had forty wives, among them two daughters of Moshweshwe. Kruger professed friendship, doubtless gave him presents and received others. The Kgatla impis pretended to help Kruger against the Basotho, though in fact Kgamanyane had an understanding with his father-in-law. But the pressure for land was insatiable.

The time came when Kgamanyane said no. The Boers declared that the presents had been an admission that they were the owners and that the Kgatla were merely tributaries paying them tax. Finally Paul Kruger, deciding to make this plain to the tribe, lured Kgosi Kgamanyane alone into a house under the pretence of friendship. After a fierce struggle he was overcome, thrown down and sjamboked. His people dared not come to the rescue of their chief, knowing it would mean his death. He was thrown back to them utterly insulted, bleeding but not conquered. He decided to take his people away from their happy land, now made so unhappy, into the harsher, drier country of the Bakwena tribe. Earlier on, the Bakgatla had helped the Bakwena against their enemies and had been promised land if they ever wanted to move. Now it was time to take up the promise.

But the Boers chased them. Kruger, with the taste of his own treachery still sour in his mouth, was not going to let Kgamanyane escape with all those cattle. Kgamanyane appealed to his brother Kgari, a rainmaker, who brought down a great storm which washed out all the tracks of people and cattle in floods of water and sand. It is said too that one of the Boers appealed to Kruger saying: 'What are we doing? Kgamanyane has done us no harm. Are we any better than cattle thieves?' And that in the end Kruger said: 'Burghers, turn your horses.'

That, then, is how Mochudi where I write, in what was Bakwena country, comes to be our capital. Not all the Kgatla people left; thousands of our cousins are still across the frontier which was drawn later on by people far off who could not have cared less how they divided families and nations of 'natives'. For all over Africa boundaries were being drawn in Chancelleries by people who knew nothing of Africa. They found it convenient to draw these boundaries along, for example, lines of latitude or rivers, ignoring the fact that the same people often live on both sides of a river valley. This is the reason why in so many cases the present boundaries of African states make utter nonsense. It is also a reason for thinking them over in a peaceful atmosphere where perhaps national boundaries drawn by foreigners in another continent will not appear to be so important. Bechuana-land, now Botswana, which was invented as a political convenience for the British is certainly a bad example. My own tribe is by no means the only one which has been split up by a frontier. In the north for instance, half the Tawana people are in Botswana and the other half are in the Caprivi strip, one of the most idiotic and irrational of the European-designed territories. It is in fact part of South West Africa, a League of Nations mandated territory now claimed by South Africa.

This is how it seems to us in Botswana. But Rhodes and his friends did not see it that way. It is important to know how they did see it but even more important to realise what Rhodes's imperial vision was bound to do to Africa and the Africans.

King Lobengula was the son of Mzilikazi. Like Mzilikazi he was a conqueror and his natural prey was the Mashona, peaceable people, remains of the great state which had once built the Zimbabwes. He and his impis would raid, take cattle, kill some Mashona and incorporate others in his armies. It seemed to be the natural order. But his kingdom stood right across the end of the 'Missionaries' Road' in the way of the man with the vision of gold in the north. It was a military kingdom, still organised more or less like Shaka's, with regiments of fighters who were now, partly at least, armed with rifles but were not trained in their use and did not perhaps understand them or believe in them as they still believed in the assegai.

And this gold, these great precious nuggets, might be anywhere at all, behind the southern boundary of Lobengula's kingdom! Prospectors and traders came north, hanging aroung Bula-1888 wayo in the smell of meat and hides and beer; each trying to get something for himself out of the king, some concession, something with a mark or with a seal. But for the future? Rhodes probably saw quite clearly that Lobengula and his kingdom must go in the interests of the British Empire. The only question was when and how. Perhaps Lobengula saw this too. At any rate he seems to have acted as though the doom was sometimes clear to him. He tried in every way to put off the day of it, to hold his people back, to get some whites, at least, on his side. He thought that at any rate John Moffat, the son of the missionary whom he had protected, would be his friend. But Moffat had his own white politicians to reckon with and besides, he too thought that Lobengula stood in the way of Christian progress.

There was a rumour that the Boers had managed to get a treaty

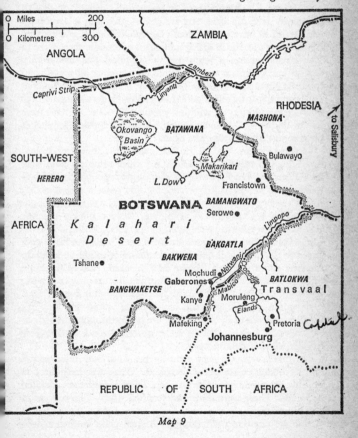

Map 9

out of Lobengula, a mining concession for themselves. It seems probable that this was a forgery or, if not, something which Lobengula and his chief minister had understood in a very different sense. Anything of the kind must have depended immensely on interpretation, not merely word for word, but the underlying sense and the future intention.

However, Rhodes managed to persuade Lobengula to disown this treaty if it did exist and instead to give him a monopoly. This seems to have been seriously agreed. The king and his successors were to be paid £100 a month and besides there were to be rifles and an armed steamer on the Zambezi. Rhodes in return was to get 'complete and exclusive charge over all metals and minerals situated and contained in my kingdom's principalities and dominions, together with full power to do all things they may deem necessary to win and procure the same'. Others were not to be allowed to come into the kingdom looking for metals or minerals. All this was quite clear.

It was of course on the surface merely a mining concession. But King Lobengula and Lotje, his chief minister, who may have been bribed by the whites—Lobengula thought so and had him and his people killed—were probably quite well aware that it was the beginning of the end for them and for Matabeleland. There was a good deal of wriggling, understandably enough. But Rhodes was already choosing his pioneers, British and Afrikaner volunteers, tough and seasoned men who would be prepared in the face of all difficulties, material or moral, to build up the new country which Rhodes had in mind. And at the same time he was drawing up the Constitution for his chartered company and striking off the phrase 'philanthropy plus five per cent' —no doubt something which most people would like. But this broad road leads to the signpost where philanthrophy and five per cent diverge and one has to make up one's mind, often rather quickly, which road to take.

Lobengula's young men were angry. They saw these whites already taking possession of their land. There was haggling and pressure from one group or another. There were letters, genuine or forged. There were shots and terrified riders. The concession was repudiated.

1890   But the pioneers went through. At one point in their march

Lobengula could almost certainly have cut them off and killed most of them. He did not do so. Perhaps he was thinking of what had happened in Zululand when Cetshwayo's first victory had been turned into defeat. And yet he was a conquering king; he could not bring himself to come into a genuine alliance with these people who were marching through his country. He saw no point in white civilisation.

The pioneers marched on. In 1890 they got to a plain of beautiful agricultural land where they decided to found Salisbury; they rapidly made a number of treaties with Mashona chiefs, who at first at any rate, were not unwilling to come under their protection and to see the tables turned on the Ndebele. But it gradually became clear that the pioneers and the Chartered Company were the real rulers of the country; they kept order. There were very few of them and a great many 'natives'. And these natives were, of course, the labour force which was necessary to ensure the success of the imperial vision. Lobengula and Matabeleland were between Rhodes and his base. It was necessary that Lobengula and the constant threat of his impis should be dealt with. The occasion of the war perhaps does not matter very much; if it had not been what it was, something else would have occurred. Rhodes and Jameson were probably pleased at the 'provocation'.

> 'What ever happened we had got
> The maxim gun and they had not.'

King Lobengula, beaten in battle, his country and its organisation fallen utterly to pieces, left his royal *kraal*, Bulawayo, to the flames of defeat, rode away and probably died of smallpox. He had no successor.

There were other rebellions. Mashona and Ndebele both tried to fight back. Both were beaten. The Chartered Company now felt secure. Rhodes's vision could become actual. White supremacy was there to stay. The twentieth century was about to dawn.

Yet it dawned differently in Bechuanaland because of the foresight and energy of a Christian King, Kgosi Khama III of the 1837-1923 Bamangwato in the north. He had been a great fighter in his time; even Mzilikazi, whom he had held at bay, admitted that. Now he was older and thought in an adult way; he realised only too clearly how his country too could be swallowed by Rhodes and become part of the territory of the British South Africa Company. With two other Batswana chiefs he went to London to plead personally with Queen Victoria for their country to remain a protectorate. This was annoying for Rhodes who wanted Bechuanaland as a jumping off place for his Uitlander plot against the Boers, (see Chapter 17) an attempt to get a bigger share of the money power of the Witwatersrand. He had been half promised what he wanted by Chamberlain, and when the three chiefs managed to get the protectorate status granted to them, he insisted on getting a strip right along the eastern edge of the territory, and cutting through the tribal territories, for his railway, part of the dream of Cape to Cairo communications, as well as several large blocks of good land which were ultimately taken over by the Crown. These Crown lands have been in turn divided up and let as farms, mostly to whites. When a tribe which has only been granted poor and arid land for its reserve wants something more, it has to pay heavily to buy back Crown land farms which used to be part of its own grazing grounds. The modern British administrator may feel that this is unfair, but the laws of a 'free economy' are too much for him. By the time the protectorate was established at the end of the nineteenth century most of the best land along the rivers, easy to water and farm profitably, was already in the possession of white farmers. So too was any potential gold-mining country. The concession by Khama of one of these blocks of coveted land meant the very brutal throwing out of a smaller, occupying tribe by their overlords. But, in today's Botswana, people are willing to forget and live for the future.

Yet what Khama did profoundly modified the inter-racial attitude, official and unofficial. The tribal reserves, though they did not include the best land, were still fairly large and could support a reasonable population. True, many of the men had to go out and work in the gold and diamond mines, but they were not positively interfered with; taxes were not adjusted so as to force them all out. A colonial power could not hope to get much out of Bechuanaland. Had it been known at the time that there were diamonds and other natural mineral resources the chiefs might not have succeeded. In those days Bechuanaland was not an investment, barely a responsibility; little of the British tax payers' money would be spent there. Up till lately the maintenance of order was the main British object and this had to be achieved as economically as possible, however much people like District Officers on the spot wanted to do more and to give help to people whom they increasingly liked and respected.

This had the effect of developing the Bechuanaland protectorate into a friendly, though dreadfully poor, society. It has to some extent allowed the moral order of the African people to adapt itself to the modern world without too much interference. Most Africans are nominally Christian, but even that has been modified, just as the gloomy Dutch Reformed Church hymn tunes have been harmonised. But the Batswana have not been oppressed. It is, perhaps, the one and only country in Africa which has become independent without hatred on either side. This is its importance and significance in today's picture of Africa. Perhaps Khama's monument, the little bronze buck on the hillside, will outlast some more expensive and elaborate ones built all over Africa to honour white empire builders.

And now, before going on, I want to look just beyond the borders of Botswana, to south-west Africa and Namaqualand. Here there were a number of people who were, in general, called the Bastars—that is, the descendants from unmarried unions between white man and slave or servant woman, but gradually back-crossing with Khoikhoi, descending in one social scale while rising in another. Chief Kido of the Witbooi 'Hottentots' of Namaqualand had a grandson, Hendrik, born in 1840, whose extant photographs show a strange racial mixture. He was a bright boy. The diary which he kept at the most active time of his life, was written sometimes in classical Dutch with copious biblical allusions, sometimes in contemporary Afrikaans.

Hundreds of the Witboois wandered, looking for a good place to settle, fighting earlier comers, mostly with the same kind of racial background. Hendrik went north from Namaqualand into the Herero country. After a win by the Herero, he was taken prisoner, but finally sent back alone on a horse. On his lonely ride he heard a 'voice' and from then on became more and more convinced that he himself was the weapon of God. From now on

1884 he was constantly fighting the Herero, at first losing, then gradually winning. He had ousted his father from the Witbooi captainship over a matter of cattle; he taunted the Herero, treating them as inferiors—'Amalakites'. The Herero answered in kind.

But then came a new situation. By 1890 the Germans had a hold on south-west Africa, based on a series of 'protection' treaties signed by the local chiefs. Kgosi Maherero signed, but Hendrik wrote to him, saying he had stupidly sold his freedom. He himself completely refused to sign and argued the meaning of the word 'protection' to unappreciative Germans who decided that, although he had in fact never injured a single white person, Hendrik Witbooi must be got rid of. They duly attacked his village, killed some seventy women and children and destroyed the houses. Hendrik and his men escaped; they were short of ammunition and he even sent to the German commander, asking for the loan of some, so as to make a fair fight. This did not appeal to the representatives of imperialism and from now on Hendrik lost all the respect for white morality which the missions had, earlier, instilled into him.

However, by 1894 the Germans had forced him to accept 'protection and friendship' which meant a German magistrate and thirty soldiers stationed in his town. He accepted this peacefully, helping the Germans to keep order elsewhere, for ten years. Then suddenly in 1904, he called up his men; something had happened, perhaps a message from the 'God', part Old Testament, part—what?—whom he imagined and who now told him to drive all the whites out of his country. Perhaps it was the same message which came to Maherero and the Nama chiefs. It was an unequal fight. Hendrik, now an old man, was forced back into the Kalahari, from which he carried on a guerilla war, but more and more people and cattle must have died of thirst every year. They killed him in the end, just as they killed the Herero leaders. It is worth remembering that the Herero rising of 1904 to 1905 ended with the death of three-quarters of the Herero and Nama. A nation of 60,000 Herero was whittled down to 16,000, with practically no cattle or means of livelihood other than working for the German farmers. General von Trotha, backed at first by Kaiser Wilhelm, who, however, under humanitarian pressure, later disowned him, had this to say : 'I believe that this nation must be destroyed as a nation . . . This uprising is no less than the first stage of a racial war . . .' The head of the German General Staff, being a logically minded man, agreed that after what had happened the enemy must be either annihilated or live 'in some sort of slavery'. They did not manage to carry through their policy as completely as they might have done, but doubtless felt that pacification had been achieved, leaving enough cheap labour to work the large farms of the settlers. There are people alive today in Namibia who remember all this very clearly. Pacification has never spelled peace.

Fourteen

Colonialism

Slowly, through the nineteenth and twentieth centuries, the European governments began to build up their colonial services. They were based on keeping order and protecting their own settlers and traders in places where they existed, but also on some kind of justice for the 'natives'. They also began to impose taxes in their own currency which usually meant that in order to pay them, most Africans had to go and work for whites, usually at extremely low wages, so that it took a long time to accumulate tax money. This was not, of course, accepted amiably by all the people; they used various methods of avoiding it; these often ended as 'native risings', after which a European government usually produced some more money for keeping order. It is not cheap or easy to collect taxes from scattered and unwilling people.

A gradual divergence began between the European administrators and those who were there to make profits. For the latter, the essential was to make the natives work, the simplest way, always, being by taxation. This method can be well studied in the Portuguese territories and also in Rhodesia, where, for the critical early years, the government was virtually the Company. The incentives which were applied to get labour were not always pleasant. People in England began to talk about forced labour; this was extremely annoying for the colonists, who said, as they have said so many times since, that they were the only people who understood their own situation and knew the right way to deal with it. In Rhodesia, as elsewhere, there was never any thought or possibility of any kind of multi-racial society. In fact, after twenty or thirty years, relations between black and white were probably worse than they were when they started. The policy of keeping down the native had been carefully and intelligently thought out and put into practice. All good land must be in the possession of the whites; native reserves must be in the less good land, so that they would have to come out and work for Europeans. When they did so they were equally segregated, this time in locations away from the pleasant white towns. There was no official *apartheid*, but whenever some individual of the Mashona or Ndebele became successful and able to compete with whites, things were made almost impossibly difficult for him. It was curious that nobody realised how brittle Rhodes's golden vision had become, how more and more inevitable and dreadful the come-back was going to be.

But in some other African countries taxes could be paid by the growing of economic crops. (It can be argued that independent African countries ought to put on heavy taxes so as to induce peasant farmers not merely to grow subsistence crops, but to grow cash crops and thus increase both the national food supply and possible exports.) Growers of economic crops often got help and advice, not only from the missionaries, but from the administrators and their expert advisers. This sometimes resulted in a comparatively high standard of living for just those people who before had never had the means of getting out of their early and often miserable conditions. They were now one up on their old rulers or conquerors and might take the opportunity of consolidating their position. It sometimes also meant real social disturbance, as, for example, when men found themselves called on to do women's work instead of fighting. In many places, they have still not made the change; the women still go on working in old and inefficient ways, without ever having the small amount of capital needed to buy better tools or seeds.

Sensible African leaders recognise this and try to give a lead. It is essential that it should be understood, because there is a tendency now in some African states and among some politicians, to put everything that has gone wrong or upset people down to white colonialism. When the colonists were farmers who wanted all the land they could grab, as most of the Voortrekkers and early Rhodesians were, then there was no peaceful coexistence possible. But probably in Kenya there could have been if it could have been thought of in time. However, with an official policy of alienating large expanses of land and the best land at that, for white occupation only, it was not possible. Yet one cannot suppose that the highly profitable tea and coffee plantations and the pedigree dairy herds of Kenya would have been possible but for white settlers. They can, no doubt, be continued now and perhaps many of them will be, as African-owned and run co-operatives, but outside capital and enthusiasm and scientific methods were needed to start them off. If only these could have gone with equal intelligence and forethought into race relations! Unfortunately that was left until too late, or, let us hope, not quite too late.

When there was administration plus trade rather than farming, as in many parts of west Africa, ordinary Africans perhaps did not pay much attention to who was, in theory, their ruler. The British administrator may well have been more just and accessible than his African predecessors, even if his justice had a different pattern and there were certain things he could not understand. Where the impact of colonialism was felt was in the lands where there was extensive white settlement, but it may well be that in some places there could have been room for all. Often a little adjustment and understanding would have made the peaceful development of both races possible. This, as I have indicated, was probably so in Kenya, though inevitably, given the political development, the white settlers were blamed for much worse than they did. Perhaps in all countries the pastoral tribes suffered most, though people who practised a fallow-and-come-back agriculture were apt to find that their fallow, grown up into bush and apparently unused, had been taken by white settlers who genuinely thought it was unoccupied.

All this took time. There were early administrators whose ideas were ahead of their time, men like George Maclean who went out to the Gold Coast in the 1830s as President of the Council of British Merchants, with few statutory powers, but tremendous goodwill and courage and great political sense. He restored moral order in places which had been shaken by the slave trade and local wars. He made peace and encouraged prosperity. His treaties, justly made, were respected. Nor was he the only one. But thoughts about order and justice followed Western thinking, often some way behind, and not necessarily including those who followed heathenish practices or stood in the way of trade.

All Europeans from the old colonialist countries must be prepared, if they are to be honest about African affairs, to do a great deal of revaluation. Those whom they were brought up to admire were not admirable from the African point of view (the same of course is true for India). It is arguable that some of the colonial powers were a lot worse than others and it was a good thing for all that they were not allowed to assert their rule as widely as they would have liked. Yet this was scarcely the motive of those who raised one flag rather than another in the process of conquest. But, people will say, they brought order, prosperity and the spread of the Gospel. Well, one has to think carefully, making sure about whose interests were involved and especially how much of the prosperity remained in Africa or was enjoyed by Africans.

Public health is comparatively recent; it is certain that, if it had not been for the necessity of keeping Europeans healthy, most of the early work on malaria, yellow fever, etc. would not have been done. Here there was a clear benefit. Yet we must remember that sleeping sickness was accidentally brought into Uganda with Lugard's Congolese soldiers, killing a vast number of people. Later doctors and scientists have tackled the African problems, not from a racial angle but out of a universal concern and, increasingly, with African colleagues. The same goes for the European professionals and technicians, citizens of the world. In a later chapter education will be dealt with more specifically.

But Africans, in a general condemnation of colonialism, must give some praise to those who worked hard to remedy injustices and bad conditions, even though they scarcely managed to step out of their European backgrounds. Men and women from Europe did brave, intelligent and generous things, perhaps for the wrong reasons or what seem to us now to be wrong reasons. Nevertheless, these things were done and are sometimes remembered in African story and song.

Colonial administrators were of course as deeply influenced by the theories of their time as everyone else. Slowly, during the Industrial Revolution, people's ideas had changed in all countries and continents. In most European countries the factory workers became voters and after that had to be considered as individuals. And with this kind of change, gradually the idea of what colonial service was, began to widen out, taking over more and more public works and public health aspects. People began to think in terms of water conservation, of new methods of agriculture, and the control of pests. The diseases which had been killers, especially in the west coast, were now under control, though it had not yet been realised that if you manage to control death, you must also control birth, or else a very difficult situation will arise. Some at least of the colonial administrative officers became more and more attached to the country where they lived and the peoples in it, especially when it became customary to learn their languages. Systems of administration began to be worked out. Much depended on whether there was a strong African king or leader and what kind of backing he had. Usually the colonial administrations, especially British, found it easier to work in with such authorities when possible and even to build them up. This tended to produce a new kind of traditionalism; the local king or chief would find himself protected and backed by the administration against those of his own people who wanted change and who were sometimes getting it, for example through new methods of trade, minor industry or agriculture and also the educated whom the administration might suppose to be dangerous. In the end it was usually worse for him because those whom he ruled might begin to think of him, once these ideas got into their heads, as the running dog of the colonialists. This was, of course, most accurate when the traditional ruler began actually to be paid by the colonial administration; he could no longer be truly integrated with his people. The council of elders and tribal meetings lost in importance compared with the white District Officer with the enormous shadowy authority of the colonial country behind him.

Nor was there uniformity (except perhaps in the minds of the Colonial Office) on what sort of authority the chiefs had. In southern Africa there was usually one son, from the Great Wife, 'born to be king'. But in other parts the chief might be chosen because of a dream or vision by some designated person. In much of the west coast the chief or king was chosen and en-stooled from among a number of possible candidates from various families; if he did not fulfil what was expected of him he could be, and often was, de-stooled. As George Moore, one of the old Ghanaian intellectuals, said : 'Sovereignty is not in the chiefs but in the people.' The Emirs of Hausaland with whom Lugard dealt (Chapter 15) were from a Moslem minority of conquerors. In some parts of Africa where there were no authorities which were recognisable to a European, chiefs were invented. And gradually a remarkable dead weight of precedents and rules and ordinances grew up in the colonial services of all nations.

However, the head posts in colonial administration became more interesting and worthwhile. And of course they mattered desperately to the inhabitants who were being administered. The result of a European war might mean a complete change in habits and standards of living for people three or four hundred miles away. The reforming German Governor of Tanganyika, Rechenburg, was, for instance, a humane and understanding man, who curbed the settlers and encouraged African farmers; his loss must have been deeply felt after that country changed hands at the end of World War I. For that matter, there are many Tanzanians now alive whose model of a soldier and leader was the brilliant and undefeated Lettow-Vorbeck.

Colonial administration and the missionaries did not always see eye to eye, especially when, as in Nyasaland, the English officials came from the English public school and upper class segment, while the Scots missionaries had a radical and sometimes working-class background. This became clear during John Chilembwe's rising in Nyasaland, although his main influence had been Booth, a Baptist believer in African equality, present before God and to be brought about before man by industrial missions which would give Africans the benefits of late nineteenth century technology. John Chilembwe, with Negro-American help, founded the Providence Industrial Mission, which almost from the beginning was looked at with suspicion by the settlers and administrators and also by other missions. This was because Chilembwe was practising what came to be known as Ethiopianism, that is to say, Christianity without whites. This kind of Christianity was looked on with more than suspicion on some of the big estates which quite simply had the African churches burnt.

Again, Africans who had begun to be successful by European standards, who had built and furnished nice houses, or who had stores or small estates, were beginning to feel desperately frustrated in a society which would only accept them as permanent inferiors. In 1915 they joined with John Chilembwe in a rising which resulted in the death of three Europeans and the serious wounding of two. But after the rising there were uncounted African deaths, men and boys shot and hanged and flogged by summary courts in an atmosphere of fear and fury, including John Gray Kufa, an Edinburgh trained African doctor, one of the 'rebels'. Any African property owners had their homes burnt and property destroyed or looted as a lesson to them. It may be noticed that the family of the manager of the worst estate, whose head was cut off, was safeguarded by Chilembwe's men. Chilembwe's church was blown up. He himself was probably killed and secretly buried, though some say the Lord God changed him into a hyena so that he could escape from his enemies; but this black-coated and trousered mission head, who was also an expert hunter, joined the ranks of the kings who died for the people (like Arthur or Barbarossa or Cleomenes in European history). People waited for him to come back. In a sense he stood by the Malawi nationalists in Gwelo prison forty years on, just as the descendants of the radical Scots missionaries stood by them in action and actuality.

But by the early years of the twentieth century most organised resistance to white occupation had died down over most of Africa. The lesson of the superior armaments had been learned the hard way. It seems as though 120,000 Africans were killed or died in 1905 the Maji-maji rebellion in German East Africa, with comparatively small white losses. This was a rising of the Bantu peoples, including many different clans and groups, against the colonialists and those whom they employed. This was the typical pattern. But the feelings of African nationhood, with all that this would mean of a different kind of resistance, were scarcely beginning yet. Towards the end of World War I when President Wilson was beginning to think out the idea that nations should control their own destinies even if they were quite small nations—and how new and strange that was at the time!—Dr. Banda was still a young student intent on his own education though no doubt he had been disturbed and influenced by the Chilembwe rising; Jomo Kenyatta, feeling his way towards politics, must have heard of it. But Nkrumah was still only a young boy, Senghor, probably at school, just beginning to learn French, while Nyerere, Kaunda, Sékou Touré and many others, were not yet born.

It may well seem that I have been over-critical of the British attitude. To be fair one must throw one's mind back to the England of the first decade of this century; a country which appeared to have immense stability of a materialistic and essentially selfish kind. As a child of that decade I felt—but how wrongly!—that I could see the whole of my life ahead of me, dull, orderly, circumscribed by upper class codes of behaviour, even though not in the vulgarly upper income group, above all safe. I did not know what forces were already eroding this solid wall of prosperity. I could not have imagined that one day I would be a member of an African tribe. Many of the English who went out to Africa went there to get away from safety and prosperity and the conventions of a class-ruled life. Many of them were looking for some kind of freedom. They were looking for romance, something to make life worth living. A few of them included the Africans in their vision of freedom, but alas, too few to be effective.

We must not, however, think of the British attitude as the only one. In French and to some extent in Portuguese colonies there was much more assimilation. The idea that the African was necessarily and always an inferior and different being was not held officially or unofficially. In French West African possessions an educated African was supposed to be becoming more and more nearly Parisian. He was an evolué; one took him seriously as an individual and a civilised being. French Africa was France; Africans in Paris represented their countries as Deputies, in cafés, in the Army and in the Communist Party. Perhaps there were not many evolués, but to have even a few of the population whose self-respect was being built up instead of being knocked down, was certainly something and it showed quickly in art and letters. Of course it is now completely unfashionable; Africans must be African, new kinds of poets and painters have appeared in the reaction against Paris. Yet those who have been in touch with the culture of France cannot help but be citizens of the world, something greater even than Africa.

The difficulty was that French colonial organisation centred so much on Paris that it became increasingly unreal to the ordinary man and woman in the French colonial territories. Whatever happened to the politicians and artists, the common man was unlikely ever to get to France and could not really see himself as a citizen of France, or a member of any of the French political parties. This was the opposite of the British theory of devolution with the centre actively pushing aside the bothers and troubles of the fringes like a rather elderly parent.

French colonial thinking certainly shocked British and German white settlers when they met it. For them the colour bar was sacred. Their code was of course simple and convenient: the whites were the employers, the blacks were the labourers. It became a little more complicated when certain kinds of skilled industrial labour became necessary and had to be highly paid and well treated. This was bound to lead to job reservation. But that was a later stage. At first in the good old days, to which settlers' romanticism looks back, there was none of that.

Perhaps one reason for this difference in attitude was that most of the African people in the French colonies were already used to peaceable trade; they knew the value of money; their homes might be almost 'civilised'. In Madagascar there was a flourishing kingdom with which the French first traded and then forced a treaty, which left the kingdom of Merina only nominally independent. The British had rather more contact with peoples who were war-inclined and did not wear the kind of clothes of which the missions approved. And yet in the end it was easier for the Africans and some British to react against the obvious injustice of their methods. French officials could not quite see what the Africans were worrying about or why, when they got the offer to become part of the French community, on apparently equal terms with Paris, they almost all refused.

But that was still far ahead. Meanwhile in the later nineteenth century rising of anti-slavery feeling was often directed against just those people amongst whom slavery as practised was not altogether evil. The slave-owning tribes in north eastern Rhodesia and Nyasaland were Moslems of a kind with some Arab mixture. Here there was no very absolute line between slave and master; plenty of talented slaves drifted upwards into the master class just as they had done in the Niger delta. This constituted a different kind of relationship between master and labourer and could not be tolerated by the British. It appeared to be immoral, both socially and economically. Hence the campaigns against it, although it must be remembered that there were also remains of the old slave-trading to the coast, as cruel as ever.

Amongst all this, far-sighted African kings and chiefs tried to make terms, often getting some missionary group or some administrator on to their side. Many of them accepted some at least of the social and technological ideas held out to them, often in spite of their more conservative counsellors. It is not easy to change a way of life or the functioning of a closed society even if you are the chief or king and can set an example or even give orders. Such things take time and meanwhile if you have good land, minerals or anything else which is enviable, you will have a host of whites prowling round your borders asking for concessions and offering bribes to you or your chief men or your wives.

King Lewanika of Barotseland, the friend and admirer of Khama, the man who refused to sell his own people to the Arab slave-traders, found himself gradually hemmed in as more and more adventurers and settlers arrived at the turn of the century. After ten years he signed letters and treaties that he would certainly not have signed earlier. Lewanika was an intelligent man and took sincerely to Christianity even when it cut across all his earlier customs. Up to a point his mission stuck by him. Yet now Barotseland finds itself left behind : if it is to prosper there will have to be changes of a kind which Lewanika could not have foreseen. In fact these are coming, in an increasingly united Zambia. But neither could the missionaries or prospectors have foreseen them.

Fifteen

Custom and Trade

While the pattern of southern Africa was shaping, as we have seen, into white domination based on skilled exploiting of natural resources, including of course, the labour force, what was happening elsewhere? We must catch up on the west coast and central Africa. But here, I believe, we should stop and think quite hard about the nature of civilisation and about the educational substructure on which civilisation depends.

When young Africans are proud of their African ancestors, as they should be, they must think very carefully before they use the word 'civilisation'. I have used it myself, I think correctly, in writing of the Sudanic kingdoms, of Ethiopia and parts of the east coast, and naturally of Egypt. It would also be permissible to think of the civilisations of the Akan and Delta states, with their gorgeous proliferation of sculpture, music and dancing, which, however it began, had developed from magic into aesthetics, though this may well be no long step. It seems probable that the original kingdom of Kongo had a civilisation, possible that there were others. But we must remember that, because people are a nation, they do not necessarily have a civilisation.

Civilisation, on whatever standard one takes it, is bound to mean something that comes with leisure: with the extra time gained, perhaps by one class only, as in many of the most advanced early civilisations—and perhaps some of the later ones—from the accumulation of food and other necessities. In this spare time the human mind can reach outward and expand its field of interest and knowledge and aesthetic delight. That way lies true freedom and the genuine security which allows people to become other-regarding, that is, altruistic.

This is no mere European definition; it would, I think, be acceptable in Asia, although in China it would have to be translated into Marxist language. I do not insist, as the Greeks might have, that civilisation implies cities. But it does imply being able to take one's mind freely off the day's food and sex, off defence from, or attack on one's neighbours or fellow animals including bacteria and viruses.

Much of Africa was not civilised by those standards. Many Africans may have had elaborate cultures, often dealing with the magic side of things. They may, like the Bushmen, have been charming people once you got to know them. But they were in no way free-minded. They could not think outside rather narrow channels of thought and feeling and could not stretch their minds to take in new concepts.

Of course, this is also true of a very high percentage of Europeans, Americans and Asians, both a hundred years ago and now. Many think along narrow, mentally enslaving channels. A technological civilisation (and without technology it is impossible to raise the standard of health or reasonable prosperity) spreads material gifts lavishly; its uncivilised citizens seize on these, thinking they have all they want or need. They can end by spoiling their civilisation, for themselves and others.

Nor do I claim that the most civilised Europeans, whose education is, as I shall point out, based on scientific modes of thinking, are incapable of taking in much that is good but different in African ways of life. The more genuinely civilised and open-minded they are, the more sympathy they should be able to have with others and the more appreciation of another philosophy. But it does not always happen. This of course is equally true of Africans who so often appear not to want to understand or sympathise with the best of European civilisation, but instead eagerly pick up the tag ends of Western grab and showing off, which are nothing to do with civilised behaviour.

What I do claim, then, is that real civilisation is always based on a rapid widening of outlook, so that there is no subject which cannot be considered and dealt with either in theory or practice. There is nothing to be afraid of. Few people of any race have really got that far; it is the aim. It is what all this machinery, all these patterns of government, all this research, all these books, are for or ought to be for, even if the aim is forgotten. In a sense none of us is civilised; we only try to be. But when the aim is even partially achieved, then one can say there is a civilisation.

But how does it come about? During the late eighteenth and nineteenth centuries the best European education became increasingly based on scientific and historical facts, in so far as they were available. These formed the basis for engineering, medical and other valuable skills, always enabling people to become more free and less afraid. Meanwhile very few Africans south of the Sahara had anything of the kind. Traditional education was suitable for traditional warfare, agriculture and justice. Certainly it made many people happy and it aimed at securing society against a number of dangers, some real and some imaginary. But it could not be a basis from which some of the real dangers, such as malaria, bilharzia, leprosy and yaws, locusts, quelea birds and cattle diseases, not to speak of recurrent droughts and floods, could be met and overcome.

On the west coast particularly, many useful European notions, especially in warfare and commerce, were picked up quickly and assimilated. Further north there was Islamic education, based on the Koran and little else except for the few who went on to the universities. In a sense this was a very decadent version of a mediaeval culture. It was not an education which could help people into the modern world. Unhappily most of the nineteenth and even twentieth century mission education was based on the Bible and on the classical education which some missionaries had. A mission educated African might have a great deal of information on Christian theology, which like Islam, was supposed to be a general guide, and a little Latin or even Greek, but nothing which would enable him to dismantle and put together an engine, still less to invent one. Nor was he introduced to such concepts as natural selection, or basic physics. Was this the educational sub-structure of civilisation? I think not. People were still afraid.

Along certain lines almost all Africans had elaborated their lives to a fantastic extent. They had made a net-work of rules which appear to the outsider to be completely unreasonable. Yet they may have made sense in terms of conduct which was moral in that it kept some kind of human cohesion and probably the moral order and belief in a collective life spirit which I have indicated earlier. So-called 'primitive' societies are often stable to a degree which people in our own unstable societies may envy. But this meant keeping rather curious rules. For example there might be only certain sorts of pattern permissible in pottery, in basketwork or weaving, in the tattooing of the right breast or the left cheek. If you followed the rules, you were US, one of the group that stuck together and whose quarrels must always be mended; if you broke them, you were THEM and so much the worse for you. But this type of culture could not accept alternatives, based not on tradition, and the net of custom, but either on force or on reason.

Many millions of people in Africa were like that. Some still are. The many peoples of the Congo interior had this kind of culture, this very elaborate non-civilisation. When it was broken the group's or tribe's cohesion broke. People were lost without the endless bustle of the rules. Some of them took as quickly as possible to other rules as laid down by missions, but found them puzzling since their rather different moral source was often incomprehensible. Other people just died because what had made living, difficult and dangerous as it was, worth while, had been removed. Above all, it had become too complicated to know who was Us, and who was Them. People struck out, blindly and brutally.

The rules and customs of such people would often seem repulsive to others, not merely Europeans but Africans from elsewhere. We can no more say all African things are good than we can say all European things are good. This is clear to the best of the African leaders, but you cannot just change people overnight. Something forbidden goes underground into the darkness of witchcraft and is used by the worst kind of people for their own power. The breaking of custom or substitution of some other kind must come from within.

In this chapter we shall look closely at what was happening in the Niger delta. It is probable that certain very dreadful things were done deliberately in front of Europeans to frighten them away. This was certainly so in Benin where the terrible mass human sacrifices were witnessed by one after another alarmed

Seventeenth to nineteenth century

and horrified European. But this means an organised state with a policy. And here the policy was 'keep out'. And it was thought out so that they could remain as middlemen between the coast and the interior, the skimmers-off of huge profits on slaves and gold. Benin did not long outlast the slave-traders as a great power. But others of the west coast states did. During the nineteenth century there was a remarkably quick adaptation from one trade to another. As in all periods of transition, when things had to be looked at in a different way, new people come to the surface and make a success of new conditions. In the palm oil trading states, thousands of pounds' worth of merchandise might go through any good trader's hands in a year; people were bound to think about the margin of profit in a modern way.

We know much more about the history here because there are abundant records, often in English. Through the century leading men had sent their sons to mission schools, not to learn religion but above all to learn to reckon quickly in whatever the measurements and currency might be. This would give them some insight into the genuine value of some of the trade goods offered to them at fantastically more than their buying price, but it would also induce them to despise their heathen parents and tell on them if this was advantageous. The traders of the Niger delta knew well that the money lay in their position as middlemen. The whites in the ships and the super-cargoes who did the trading were now able to live for long periods on the coast and survived, thanks mostly to quinine. The heads of the Houses, the great trading establishments, kept up friendly relations with an eye to mutual advantages. There was, of course, always friction; English and African law might regard offences differently; while a punishment that seemed reasonable in one culture, was deeply resented by another.

The Houses in all the city states were part slave and part free, but intelligence and good trading could take a man quickly up the ladder. However, birth counted at the top positions and in many cities the slaves united against oppression or injustice. These revolts, which began in the third quarter of the nineteenth century, disturbed trade, and the British Consul and those he represented sided with the respectable, the slave owners. But there was one slave who was going to make the grade. This was Jubo

Jubogha usually known as Ja Ja. He was an Ibo with all the qualities of his nation, a proud and rebellious boy who managed in the House of Anna Pepple to show his ability and to get on to the first step. At thirty he was a young trader, respected for his integrity and quick decisions. But he did not take sides too obviously when King Pepple of Bonny was involved in civil war and was succeeded by a young anti-traditionalist son, George, who was no fighter and tended to quarrel with his own chiefs, who at one time even deposed him.

Yet when it came to electing the new head of the House of 1863 Anna Pepple, it was Ja Ja who was chosen before older and perhaps richer chiefs. (The anglicised names may seem curious but are how they were written at the time.) His Arabian Nights type of rise excited the romantic Burton, at that time British Consul. It seems as though Ja Ja hated the political intriguing of Bonny. It may well have been a decadent and unattractive court and perhaps Ja Ja prided himself on being Bush and above such things. It is clear from the fact of his success that he was able to think in the complicated terms of relatively modern trade. He may even have set his face against 'dash', the elaborate system of present-giving which still survives and makes frequent awkwardness, since it turns so easily into corruption. What is suitable for a chief is not suitable for a merchant, still less a civil servant. Could Ja Ja have seen this far? He seems to have adapted completely to the patterns of commerce. He made friends with the chiefs of the interior and was probably quite aware of what the whites wanted and ultimately got—complete control of the navigable Niger, either by conquest or by treaty.

But Ja Ja stood in the way. He had many supporters; any able and honest trader, free or slave, had his backing. The time was to come when he would need this, for the other great House of Bonny, Manilla Pepple, was piling up armaments, guns and gunpowder, and war canoes armed with guns and cannon.

Yet Oko Jumbo, head of the other House, was sufficiently modern not to want to ruin Ja Ja, but simply to keep him down. However, Ja Ja retired with all his people and founded a new state which cut off Bonny from the oil producers. The British traders took sides according to their interest, selling arms to both. In 1870, Ja Ja proclaimed his new kingdom as Opobo. Most of the Ibos followed him and Bonny gradually declined as a trading state while Opobo progressively flourished.

For a long time King Ja Ja stood between the interior and the European powers. But the young King George Pepple I of Bonny, educated in England, reader of *The Times* and enthusiastic supporter of the missions, saw further ahead than his rival of Opobo; his wider contacts beyond Africa showed him what was bound to happen and where it was wise to choose his side. In the end his side won.

Ja Ja's stubborn power became too much for Sir Harry Johnston, then Acting Consul, and for that matter the Foreign Office in London (though not for the Foreign Secretary Lord Salisbury who, irritatingly enough for Johnston, kept on thinking of King Ja Ja as a respectable reigning monarch). There were deliber-
1887 ately misleading messages. Ja Ja surrendered and was duly humiliated. There was no more obstacle either to evangelisation or to trade. The oracles became dumb. Bonny prospered.

For a long time the various city states of the delta had been desultorily at war with one another and at first used the missions and white traders for their own ends. But this did not work out. The missions became more arrogant and insisted on 'protection'. The particularly heathenish old town of Calabar was wiped out 'in the most able manner' by the British Navy in 1855. And over the next thirty or forty years, the city states were broken up, their whole systems of administration, which of course were bound up with the state religion, were done away with, their customs, at any rate in the areas which the missions and their protectors controlled, were abolished. Nor should one forget the singularly uncharitable young white missionaries who hounded to his death the eighty-year-old, but black, Bishop Crowther of the Niger mission.

Trade was now booming, for the winners. The United African Company, formed in 1879 under Sir George Goldie, was busily making treaties further and further north with chiefs, who could always be induced to cede territory and confer monopolies. African independent traders some of whom, perhaps, had not stuck to the highest standards of Manchester, were crowded out. The missions flourished, breaking new ground and coming in greater variety. They were all so busy on the Niger that they scarcely noticed the influx of German merchants into the Cameroons and Togo. Here Bismarck struck suddenly, getting a piece of empire for Germany before it was too late.

But everywhere along the west coast of Africa, European settlements were becoming more durable. As trade increased and diversified it gradually turned from a process of keeping order into a government. In the 1870s the Dutch decided to pull out. But the French, as we have seen, were exploring and spreading spheres of influence and trade right through the territories of the old central empires.

Education on several different levels was spreading on the west coast of Africa. So were various forms of Christianity; some of the stranger American varieties of religion took root there and became even stranger. Meanwhile, more economic crops were successfully grown. Both the English and French colonies became so-to-speak paying concerns. But the better health conditions brought out whole European families and this began to mean social cleavage. In the interior there was still slavery and little progress in any sense. Unhappily many bad mistakes were made, often against the advice of the British administrators on the spot or in neighbouring territories. For instance, in Sierra Leone, by the late years of the nineteenth century the educated creoles—the native-born sons and daughters, or by now grandsons and grand-daughters, of the returned American ex-slaves—were members of all the professions : doctors, teachers, administrators and so on. It was virtually their country. But the blame was put on them for various disturbances and minor wars. As always and as we have seen lately in the Congo, the death of one white missionary appeared to matter far more than the death of a hundred Africans. A new slant in British policy almost succeeded in keeping the creoles out of medicine and the higher posts in law and administration. It was the old dislike of the 'educated native' in a new form.

This was to be equally clear in other parts of the British ruled west coast. For instance, some of the old Ghanaian families, originally descendants of 'mixed' marriages, had produced not only intellectuals, but administrators who rose to high positions. Some of them were perhaps rather conservative, but it was not because of this that, after the end of the nineteenth century, they were no longer candidates for top jobs. The new imperialism, conceived in Birmingham, had no room for them.

Meanwhile, any British advance towards the interior was held up by the Ashanti. There was a series of wars and little attempt to come to any kind of terms on which the two peoples could live peacefully together. At first the British were defeated, but gradually modern weapons began to tell. Kumasi of the patterned walls and golden furnishings was wrecked and looted. Highly treacherous dealings with the Asantahene, his relations and followers, seemed justified to the British. After all, they were natives and British military honour was at stake! It was not until well into the twentieth century that any kind of compromise was reached which would leave this people with some of their essential patterns of customs and culture. And then it was perhaps too late. The reason why the compromise was made may have been because the soldiers or their officers wanted to understand the Ashanti people who had stood up to them so impressively, whose discipline and courage and military tactics were those of a 'civilised' nation. A young soldier anthropologist, Rattray, went out in a different spirit to anything which had moved administrators before his time. It is clear from his book that he was, so to speak, converted. The Ashanti way of life and moral order, explained to him by those to whom he listened as no white man had ever listened before, overwhelmed Rattray and induced him to write almost as one of them.

Nor had the Ashanti kingdom been the only one to make trouble. In 1871 the chiefs of the small coastal kingdoms, led by King Ghartey IV of Winneba, had come together to form the Fanti Confederation. This object was to build a modern state which would both be powerful enough to stand up to the Ashanti, and also would develop all the resources, mineral and agricultural, of the country, introduce industries and establish schools. There was to be a Representative Assembly and the many west coast intellectuals, quite a number of whom came from or married into royal houses, were to be drawn in. The Confederation was not anti-British, but it would have stopped further British control and commercial exploitation. So the Confederation was declared unlawful, the ministers arrested and the area of the small kingdoms was made into a new British Crown Colony.

But the European powers were morally uneasy. At the Berlin conference in 1885, they produced a set of excellent moral intentions to justify the extension of their rule in Africa. This ultimately became the theory of the Dual Mandate. One part of the Mandate was to stop the slave-trade and kindred evils and to bring in instead the material and moral benefits of their own civilisation. On the other hand, the trade and resources of Africa must be made available to the rest of the world. And of course, this could be interpreted with varying emphasis. Sir Frederick Lugard was Administrator in Northern Nigeria, even then culturally and religiously very different from the rest of Nigeria. The Ibos in the east, the Yoruba in the west, with various smaller groups who had definite personalities of their own, as well as a middle belt of less settled people, were each as different as, say, Spaniards and Swedes. He thought out the system of indirect rule. It certainly seemed to make administrative sense in Northern Nigeria with its large population and existing government, and it appealed to the home Government as being cheap. The Fulani Emirs through whom he worked already kept order, administered justice and collected taxes. It was relatively simple to add to this a network of British residents who could suggest or even enforce improvement and check obvious tyranny and injustice by virtue of the force behind them. This meant that on the whole, Lugard and his successors got the ruling classes on their side, and for a time this seemed adequate and was copied in other parts of Africa, but it did not allow for the coming to the surface of new forces or for what education and technical progress would do to change old patterns of rule.

As technical progress in the exploiting of raw materials went on in the twentieth century, so west Africa and especially the Gold Coast, became potentially very rich, though for many years most of the profits of the exploiting companies went back to Europe or America. There was rubber, gold, manganese, bauxite and diamonds. The heavy ores needed railways and ports and gave a great deal of employment. Then came cocoa which soon, together with the still important palm oil, provided millions of pounds in export.

Labour conditions in large scale industries on plantations might be very bad and occasionally led to scandals; but how else could the profits flowing in to shareholders be kept so high? The same kind of thing was happening in many parts of the world, especially perhaps South America. Cocoa, however (brought to Ghana as recently as 1879 by a Ghanaian blacksmith) remained almost entirely an African farmers' crop. Perhaps that is why world cocoa prices have swung so disastrously; there were no white interests to placate among the primary producers.

Nigeria was only a little behind the Gold Coast and so were the French territories. All this affected not only people's pockets but their ideas. One cannot meet the full impact of the modern world of money values and apparently universal know-how and still keep one's old customs and reverences. Fundamental Christian beliefs did not necessarily conflict in the same way since many of them only expressed familiar concepts in other forms. But the ideology of capitalism quickly brought out the ideology of anti-capitalism. Nor can one educate without putting ideas into the heads of one's pupils. These ideas included freedom, nationalism and the importance of the individual personality and dignity. It was not accidental that the first of the British Commonwealth African states to become independent was also the richest: Ghana.

Sixteen

North Africa and Ethiopia

North Africa along the Mediterranean coast, that is to say the Maghreb, was a Moslem culture, though sometimes with influences from other religions. It had been governed from Istanbul, but during the nineteenth century the Turkish Empire was gradually losing out, mostly, perhaps, because of corruption and inefficiency at the centre. Whoever was said to rule, and nominally Tripoli, Tunis and Algiers were Ottoman possessions, the European powers were coming to regard the southern fringe of the Mediterranean as a series of territories where they could play power politics against one another, in the interests of trade, naval bases or simply for prestige. Morocco was still an independent country in the first half of the nineteenth century. The Sultans firmly stuck to their lucrative slave trade, at the same time restricting contacts between their citizens and Christians.

This was the position when the French invaded Algiers, on a 1830 rather flimsy excuse, partly perhaps to counter British influence in Tripoli and Tunis and partly to take the minds of the French people off their own misgovernment. They conquered and held the coastal towns, making use of the existing jealousy and bad feeling between townspeople and peasants. During twenty years of brutal campaigning, which shamed their own intelligentsia, as the last war of liberation shamed their grandchildren, they were unable to subdue these peasants in the hilly, difficult interior. The next step was colonisation, mostly by small farmers from the south of France who had been unable to make a success of their vines and olives there. They were hardly the kind to have any sympathy with or understanding of the *indigènes*. In the usual colonial pattern they were settled, some 100,000 of them, 1847 in the more fertile parts of Algeria along the coast; some of them certainly did well, bringing back into cultivation land which had been without corn or oil or wine since Roman times. The coastal towns filled up with other southern Mediterranean people, mostly small traders hoping to make a bit out of a new prospect. The peasants, driven out of their lands, never accepted the situation, and as the unpleasant realities of colonisation were forced on them the Algerians in the coastal towns who had been comparatively well treated, began to be increasingly resentful.

In Morocco the Sultans survived, but France and Spain growled at one another over them. Equally, in Tripoli, the British supported one pasha, the French another. There was a considerable Islamic revival here, and the slave trade remained, almost as an act of defiance. Tunis, the most progressive and commercially successful state of the Maghreb, was also held in an uneasy political balance, but finally succumbed to French forces and a treaty which established the paramountcy of France, though luckily it did not bring quite so many colonists as in Algiers.

Thus things went on uneasily during the nineteenth and early twentieth centuries. In 1911 Italy joined the scramble, rather late, attacking at the nearest point, Tripoli. But the Moslem tribesmen resisted to the end. The Italian army next took a bite at Eritrea. Then Morocco was partitioned between France and Spain, the former taking the larger part. Yet in a sense Morocco was lucky, since for thirteen years it had as its Resident General, a man who was in deep sympathy with the best of Islam and who felt that tradition must be gently changed, not broken— Marshal Lyautey. He ruled, much as Lugard did in west Africa through the Sultan and the cadis, but always with tact and sensibility. He managed to bring law and order far beyond any territories that any sultan had controlled. Yet it may be that the system of indirect rule put too little pressure on to some traditional rulers whose methods and tempers were so peculiarly horrible that one cannot imagine anything but relief from their subjects when they were killed or otherwise brought under control.

Spanish rule in northern Morocco was successfully attacked by 1921 Abd el Krim, leading the mountain Berbers. But the French army was too much for him, though Lyautey gave him the treatment of an honourable foe.

But resistance movements and leaders were constantly appearing throughout the Maghreb, some based on Islamic revivals, but, as the years went by, increasingly influenced by European political ideas, first found in school text books and later, perhaps, at Universities in France and elsewhere. Political and Islamic ideas were combined in the Pan-Islamic movement which sought to iron out local or regional differences in face of the very real menace of supposedly, if not genuinely, Christian Europe.

By 1900 there were more than half a million French colonists in Algiers, but the Moslem population had grown too. Naturally they got the worst jobs and the worst pay. No colour bar and rapid assimilation were fine in theory, but the practice was different. Political groupings became apparent. In Morocco a young sultan had been chosen by the French, as malleable material to educate in their way; they counted on using him to counter anti-French propaganda among his people. But Sidi Muhammad's (Mohamed V) French education made him a nationalist, although for a time he pretended to play the conquerors' game. Tunis had a respectable middle-class nationalist political party, the Destour, just as Egypt had a respectable party, the Wafd. But neither of these really represented the ordinary people of the country. Both were superseded, though both had their effect in developing informed nationalist feeling.

We must remember that racially none of these north African countries was Negro, though doubtless there was always some Negro admixture through trade and slavery. Arabic was a common language. As with Egypt, the natural pull to which all the countries along the African edge of the Mediterranean respond is rather from the east than from the south. It was from Mecca that their first conquering civilisation came, Mecca to which they still looked. Yet they are also in the Mediterranean ambience of political thought, social and trade relations.

But as communications become quicker and political aspirations clearer, the Maghreb has been increasingly conscious of and important to the great mass of Africa south of the Sahara. Their full-blown independence is very important for help and encouragement to the African countries which are still struggling.

However, that is for today. Meanwhile we must go back to the Sudan in the mid-nineteenth century. Racially, it was not a single country. There were 'pagan' Negro tribes in the south related to the peoples of northern Uganda, while in the north people were basically Moslem Arabs, although here too there was considerable admixture. Slave-raiding was always going on, yet Moslem pilgrims, mostly from western Africa, were always crossing the Sudan, always hospitably received. There were several different cultures here but not yet by the mid-nineteenth century a nation, or even two nations, only different degrees of rule or power and a great many people completely escaping from any central control. In fact it is one of the cases where it is difficult to see how the present boundaries can ever enclose a unified nation with the same interests, unless people become so exhausted from struggling and fighting with one another that they can agree at least for a time. And, during the period of amnesty, education and economic interest may exert their slow pressure against religious and cultural irrationality and for peace. But this cannot happen if armed Moslem troops are turned loose on 'pagan' villages for a private and horrible *jihad*. During the period we are considering, the Turks in Egypt exerted continual pressure and in fact Sudanese history over the last century and a half has been one of reaction in one form and another against Egypt but always with a wary eye on Ethiopia, their neighbour on the south-east.

It was the pressure of Egypt and the Egyptian appointed soldiers and administrators that led to the rise of the Mahdia. It was of course Turkish-ruled Egypt at that time but it had broken away increasingly from the Turkish Empire of which Istanbul had so long been the centre. When the slave trade was, if not ended, at least very considerably discouraged, it was done so as to suit Egyptian policy and in fact it upset the whole economy of the Sudan. It was accompanied by new and heavier taxes. The 1873 irritation and anger this caused in the Sudan was made all the fiercer because, as was mentioned in an earlier chapter, the Khedive had appointed a European Christian, General Gordon, as Governor. This inevitably meant that his country, England, was brought in when he was in danger.

The Mahdi himself was not only the gathering point for Sudanese hatred of Egypt, the leader they needed, but also he was a religious reformer. He was the one expected and at last shown forth, the possessor of the divine secret. There have been

other, lesser, Mahdis, following the same pattern of prophecy.
But he was the great one. He led his armies against the Turks,
who, although Moslems, had lapsed from the true faith revealed
to the Mahdists. The garrison at Khartoum could not hope to
stand against them; Gordon was sent to evacuate it, but dis-
obeyed orders. The Mahdi's men killed him on the staircase of
the palace of Khartoum while England and much of the west of
Europe waited in tense anxiety for news. The killing had been
against the Mahdi's orders, but men in furious religious wars
forget orders for mercy; one fears that this still happens.

Both Gordon and the Mahdi died in the same year, 1885,
though in a sense the Mahdi went on living since the chosen of
God does not die. After his death there was chaos and discouragement, the Arab clans struggling against one another and an
occasional terrible famine, for much of the Sudan is the kind of
dry country where an inch or two less rain means crop failure.
The British, taking the place of the Khedives, reconquered the
Sudan and here again one sees the pattern of a well-meaning,
hard worked, British District Officer or District Commissioner
working, usually alone, to keep order and administer some kind
of justice, dying of fever or suddenly speared, but certainly loved
and mourned by some. Later he was replaced by a different kind
of administration. In the Sudan of today one finds the great
cotton-growing schemes, the irrigation and careful cultivation
which with luck survives speeches of politicians and changes of
government, not to speak of new and unforeseen cotton diseases
and parasites.

In Egypt itself British occupation went on complacently with
the control of the Suez canal and the way to India. But here
again forces were at work which would break through, although
not immediately.

It is not good for a country's morale to have any kind of long-
term foreign occupation. The worst sort of people, the crawlers
and those with petty ambitions, get to the top. This is particularly so for a partly-educated country with an ancient and very
real civilisation of its own, where less educated and sometimes less
civilised men and women of the occupying power are put into
a superior position. All this seems commonplace now, but it had
to be learned the hard way.

But the empire of Ethiopia remained independent. It had always had some contacts with Europe and developed its own versions of religion, the arts and administration. It was essentially the land of the Amhara, a country of Christian fasts and feasts, sometimes not recognisable to the visitor from north of the Mediterranean, but also of magic squares and patterns with Judaic affinities. Here were obelisks and thrones and monasteries whose large and splendid illuminated manuscripts must have accounted for hundreds of goats who contributed the best part of their skins to be written on.

Yet perhaps the best of these manuscripts are in London or Paris. For there were rich explorers and collectors as well as punitive expeditions, above all the British one which had ended in the storming of Magdala and the death of the Emperor Theo-
1867 dore. As ever in Africa there had been misunderstandings, happenings which looked like treachery to one side, good sense to the other.

The Emperor Theodore's successor, John, had his hands full, largely with the threat of invasion from Egypt. Here religion came in, for the invaders were of course Moslems. There were other wars with the southern tribes, especially the Galla, and with the Moslem Somali along the coast, where the object was to get a seaport. These more or less conquered people were worse treated than the Amharic peasants, who themselves bore the heaviest burden of taxation, which was used for the upkeep of church, army and court.

Meanwhile Italy too had become a colonial power, though late into the scramble. At the time when the Mahdi seemed most powerful in the Sudan, Italian expeditions were feeling their way inland from Eritrea. John's successor, the Emperor Menelik, signed a treaty with the Italians which was in itself the beginning of further misunderstandings and finally war. In the end
1896 the Italians were beaten by Ras Makonnen at Adowa with an enthusiastic and united Ethiopian army. Eritrea was left to them but the defeat rankled and at last blew up hideously in the minds of Mussolini and his fascists who were prepared to go to all lengths to crush these blacks who had defeated their fathers.

The Emperor Menelik and his able Empress Taitu did their best to safeguard by treaties and arrangements this rather awkwardly placed kingdom of theirs which had no seaport. And the Emperor went cautiously ahead with internal reforms; the idea of Ethiopia as a modern state was beginning to take shape in a few minds. He was succeeded by the able and well-educated Governor of Harar, the young Ras Tafari, as Regent, ruling at first in conjunction with the rather conservative but peace-loving Empress Zawditu, Menelik's middle-aged daughter. But when she died in 1930 Ras Tafari was crowned Emperor at Addis Ababa and took as his name Haile Selassie—Might of the Trinity. He was to need all the might he could call on and all his own intelligence and all that education and natural nobility can give to a man in the years which followed, in Geneva at the League **1935** of Nations, in exile, at last on his return when in the moment of victory he insisted on giving back good for evil. Yet this, admirable though it was, cannot be enough in a modern state. Feudalism has had its day. Ethiopia must move on.

It looks as though the attitude towards land in most of Ethiopia was rather different from that in southern Africa. Land tends to be thought of not perhaps as belonging to individuals, but certainly to kinship groups. This seems to be the attitude in much of northern Africa, as far south as Kenya. Is this something which is likely to follow a settling down and change first from a wandering pastoral life to crop-growing, and then to more modern farming methods with farmers planning ahead and needing more security? That may be the general tendency. Perhaps there is an answer half-way between common ownership of land which often means difficulties in modernisation, and individual ownership with the unfortunate consequences that this usually brings with it—either fragmentation or large estates and landless peasants. Today various forms of co-operation are being tried out in different parts of Africa; one would certainly not expect the same organisation to work everywhere.

Somalia is another African country which has its own special problems. Its people are Moslem and of northern stock, organised in clan families and with no feelings of brotherhood towards their Negro African neighbours from the south, nor, for that matter, towards their Ethiopian neighbours on the west, who over the centuries were constantly edging in on them. Their history is one of fighting, with all the loyalties which this engenders.

Their genealogies go back to the time of the Prophet, which may, in itself, turn their eyes towards the past.

They too fell into the various spheres of European influence. Had their country not been so dry and difficult and poor, no doubt the Europeans would have found it a more attractive prize, spent more money on it and occupied it more effectively. But it did not seem even to have minerals. It was left alone to become a new kind of difficulty for another kind of state.

Seventeen

Gold, Diamonds, Blood

Meanwhile the century dragged to its end in South Africa. For thirty years the two kinds of whites, the Boers or Afrikaners, and the British, had struggled with one another for power, though constantly the reasonable people on both sides were trying to make peace and achieve some kind of federation—white federation of course. It would have been bad enough without the gold and diamond mines. With these extremely glittering prizes to plot and fight for and with the kind of men who are attracted to the quick profits and violence—the romance if you will—of gold and diamond mining, things were that much worse. Nobody trusted anyone else. Above all it was impossible for Africans and whites to trust one another. Judges and missionaries were involved, often against their will, in politics.

Whatever happened the Africans lost. Dinizulu, Cetshwayo's son, tried to get back his father's lands and was approached by a combination of British and Boers who established him as king and then demanded as their price so many full size farms that 1884 they would have taken up three-quarters of Zululand had they been given what they wanted. In the end they compromised rather angrily for half.

This process, repeated everywhere, broke the chiefdoms and their moral order. People saw their kings and chiefs beaten in war, humiliated and made to make shameful promises, sometimes betraying them for the sake of a glittering government prize. It seemed no use any longer going through initiation. Who cared now for the beautiful oxhide shield? Better to go and work for the whites, come back with a sixpenny knife, a bottle of scent, a pair of trousers, a few swear words and perhaps a dose of the white's illness. Only in the protectorates could the chiefdoms still function as a social entity although circumscribed by mission prohibitions. But even here bribes and pressures came over the frontiers, especially in a Protectorate such as Swaziland with valuable natural resources.

By 1895 Rhodes had already had four years as Prime Minister of Cape Colony, the British nexus of the southern African countries with the various protectorates and spheres of influence extending north to Salisbury and beyond, so that the imperial dream was half fulfilled. He was also building railways, buying out rivals or foreigners and pressing on in several different and profitable directions. He had dealt with most of his political enemies and had immense financial and newspaper power, probably far too much for any normal person to cope with and keep any moral judgement. Many people in Africa and England were getting rich in his wake; a new class was emerging. It is difficult to know how much money was leaving Africa. In and around the gold and diamond mines accurate statistics are often difficult to come by. We do, however, happen to know what the much simpler situation was in the northern Rhodesian copper belt in 1949. Here only one-third of the total of £36.7 million, which was the value of the output of copper, was actually spent in northern Rhodesia and that includes taxes and European wages and salaries—the largest bit of the third.

But it is probably true to say that unless the Europeans had come the gold would mostly have stayed underground. The diamonds would have lain unnoticed in the fields. That might have been better for everyone.

As the months went by the tension grew between Kruger and his Boers and the Uitlanders—the British who had only been given what they considered most inadequate rights in the Transvaal. Rhodes's plan was an armed rising which would be welcomed warmly by those whose feelings had been worked up. It would have a 'rescue our women and children' motto. Then the British flag would be raised, Kruger's dominance would be broken, and he, Rhodes, would be Premier of a vast South Africa, part of the imperial dream.

> 'Wider still and wider, may thy bounds be set.
> God who made thee mighty, make thee mightier yet.'

But things went wrong. Although his lieutenant Jameson was busy drilling raiders in his Bechuanaland base, the centre of the plot had come unstuck. Some of the men in Johannesburg who should have been leading the rising got cold feet. Then Jameson decided he couldn't wait any longer and rode across the border into the Transvaal with five hundred men. It was a complete 1895 failure. Kruger ended as the winner. The reasonable people saw all their hopes of a peaceable compromise put back a generation. The European powers quivered with anger against one another. There were telegrams. There were almost 'incidents'; Britain's moral prestige dropped, Rhodes's day was over. He could no longer be Prime Minister. His comment was : 'Well, it is a little history being made. That is all.' But he said it in bitter distress. Some of the directors of the British South Africa Company resigned, the shares fell, everything seemed to break. And yet Rhodes as a man survived. It was immediately after this that he went unarmed into the Matopos and talked the Matabele chiefs who had led the rising into submission. The strange power, the golden tongue, survived.

Joseph Chamberlain was the paramount influence in English politics; whether or not he knew anything beforehand of Rhodes's plans, he was a man of the same kind, an imperialist. Kruger in Pretoria was old and angry. Milner was High Commissioner; he also was an imperialist, but a more cautious one. Shares were going up; the Rhodesian gold mines had come into production. Great Britain was in a fairly good position with the other European powers who had simmered down. The Transvaal government and the Uitlanders quarrelled more and more fiercely. Newspapers published articles. Troops were mobilised. In 1899 the South African War began.

There was a strong body of sympathisers with the brave Boer farmers all over Europe, not least in England where men like Lloyd George and for that matter my own father, risked slander and disgrace, sometimes risked their lives, to attack imperialism and as they saw it, money power, mammon itself, which was trying to crush a small independent state of poor but honest people. In their picture of the war the 'native' had little part. This is abundantly clear, for instance, in Kipling's Boer War stories. Africans who had fought side by side with the British against the common enemy could not understand why their allies showed no friendliness or gratitude.

In 1902 the war was over and Milner planning a settlement which would mean real peace between the two white nations. But he was never in genuine sympathy with the Boers; with his background it would have been impossible. It would probably have been as repugnant to him and to his like among the English upper classes to sympathise with the savage Boers as with the savage natives. It was not people like Milner who could talk to Botha and Smuts; that must wait for a less aristocratic generation of English (and Scottish) politicians. Nor was genuine peace an easy idea. There had been deeply painful episodes, especially the British concentration camps, where many Boer women and children died, which would leave the kind of memories which stay alive in popular imagination.

However, there were very real attempts at reconstruction and reconciliation between British and Boers. Nobody knew or cared how many Africans had died in their war. A huge loan was raised. The only difficulty was that the mines were not working fully because of a labour shortage. This was met by the importation of industrious Chinese. It could no doubt have been met by raising African mine wages, but what would the farmers have said to that? By now in South Africa almost all the good, easily-worked land where there was adequate rainfall was in white hands. The Africans were being pushed back into 'reserves' which could not possibly support a population which grew all the more because war and war-training was no longer allowed, but perhaps dropped in quality. The men had to go off and look for work. There were dozens of them after every job, so the farmers could pay as little as would keep their labour alive. It was a simple economic situation and it was repeated in most parts of Africa when conditions were such that Europeans could colonise.

It was made worse by the fact that in South Africa and Rhodesia at least, an individual white farmer usually took over a very large tract of land, sometimes so large that it could be worked in the most primitive and wasteful way without fertilisers, but depending on a natural fallow. And again a tract of land might be taken up by a farmer because it had 'natives' on it who would naturally work for him in return for not being thrown out. The more ignorant of them might, in return, consider him as a kind of chief to whom they must transfer their allegiance. This was the old, patriarchal Trek-Boer pattern.

For certain crops (for instance tea, cotton or carefully irrigated citrus) a large area is sensible and economic. Other crops, such as coffee, can be grown by individuals but they must work together as a co-operative in drying the berries. The same holds for many other crops which need processing. It works admirably on the coast of Africa for the basic cocoa and oil nut farming. But in many African countries, Europeans came out, perhaps without much capital, or even the knowledge that was needed for agricultural improvement and got by because they could get a huge piece of land and plenty of badly-paid or even unpaid workers.

It is in this kind of situation that the doctrine of *baasskap* (white domination) and *apartheid* grows up. In South Africa, it was in essence purely economic, a means of ensuring a supply of labour. But of course, it was built up through sentiment, religion and a distorted view of history. If political *apartheid,* essentially a doctrine of separate states of African and European origin, had been worked out fairly from the beginning, with an equitable distribution of land and the natural resources which went with the land, it could have worked. Perhaps some of those who thought it out as a philosophy intended this, but political pressure made it impossible. In fact it seems doubtful at the moment whether a genuinely multi-racial state will work in to-day's Africa : perhaps later on. But by the time it was thought of seriously, there was no good land left, only the over-populated, eroded, dry areas which are today designated or about to be designated as Bantustans. All the mineral resources with their attached industries, the good seaports and so on, are in the white areas. And to the political aspect of *apartheid* has been attached all the odious social aspects, many of which are designed to further *baasskap,* the perpetual domination of the whites who are intent on not allowing Africans to reach educational or commercial levels where they can compete. But we must remember that in a sense every time a modern African state turns out its Europeans or makes things too uncomfortable for them to live there, it too is practising a kind of *apartheid.*

But in South Africa, policies which are now clear-cut were still not thought out fifty years ago. Rapid industrialisation was bringing its own difficulties. As the gold and diamond mines developed, complex engineering and geological problems presented themselves and had to be solved. But prosperity continued and more gold poured out of the mines. Rhodes founded his Rhodes scholarships at Oxford and might have done wiser things as he grew old. 1902 But he died.

There were other currents beginning. In the Cape, there was by now a large population of Coloureds, people of mixed ancestry, the descendants of white settlers and Khoikhoi or even Xhosa as well as Malay or Indian wives or mistresses; in fact everyone except the pure-bred European wives. They had built up their own communities and with prosperity and education were generally accepted though usually in rather inferior jobs or professions. But a Coloured man was not debarred from voting and there was no theoretical bar to any rise in society or even inter-marriage. But beyond the Cape, things were not so good. The somewhat conservative African People's Organisation came into existence to stand by Coloured people in South Africa beyond the Cape and to bring them the political and social advantages which the Cape Coloureds still had. By now the last Zulu rebellion was 1906 crushed and Dinizulu imprisoned for four years in spite of his defence by the brother of the influential writer Olive Schreiner.

Mohandas Gandhi was one of the many Indians who had come out to Africa. He had a good practice at the Natal bar. But he had been reading Tolstoy and now he was making up his mind to throw up all his prospects and organise passive resistance against the oppression of the Indians who had come out as indentured labourers and settled in the Transvaal. The beginnings of Indian freedom happened in Africa. But Gandhi, who organised an ambulance service with the British in the Zulu rising of 1906, does not seem to have noticed the oppression of Africans. However his followers have done so and stood nobly by their fellow non-whites.

The first Bantu newspaper IMVO started in 1884. It was edited by John Jabavu, founder of a famous family, but a weak man when, later on, it came to standing up for fundamental rights. Yet it was a beginning.

By the early years of the twentieth century, there were African political leaders in the modern sense. All they wanted were the most moderate reforms and recognition, and cautiously, timidly perhaps 'to advance the general prosperity and progress of the country and its people'. When the Southern African Native National Congress was founded in 1912 by men like Dube, Seme and Plaatje, it did not perhaps seem so very important. But one woman saw this clearly: Harriette Colenso, daughter of the Bishop, then about my own age, financially ruined through her efforts to defend Dinizulu. She wrote to Dube that the Bantu 'have now found their voice'. That voice would grow stronger, joined by other voices. But it was the first move.

Soon after the war an immensely conciliatory and liberal legislative union of South Africa under the British Crown was carried. The Cape delegates tried very hard to get the same franchise for coloured men (it was before the days when women had a vote anywhere, though they were struggling for it in England) in other parts of the Union. In fact they, and indeed several enlightened Afrikaner politicians, looked forward to a vote for everyone with 'civilisation' whatever their race or colour.

Why, when so many people meant so well, did things go wrong? There was an immense spread of African education, schools and colleges. Universities were thrown open to all. Opportunities for getting on professionally and socially seemed to be growing, though mostly for the African urban middle class who had at least got a foot in the lower ranks of the professions and had, most of them, taken to European each-for-himself capitalism, and the social rat-race that went with it.

Of course there were bad social pockets; there was the incredibly reactionary and short-sighted South African Labour Party whose name still muddles progressive people in England. Its aims were, simply enough, to keep up the wages of skilled whites. Here they were very successful; the wages of these skilled (white) workers were up to ten times the wages of unskilled (black) workers. The difference was still greater in the northern Rhodesian copper mines. This was the pattern to be hammered home by the Job Reservation Act which ensured that all highly-paid work was to be done by white labour. With this difference in wage structure, there could, of course, be no working class solidarity. Black and white workers were two entirely different classes. Nothing since has altered this.

There was always, allied to this, the underlying idea in South Africa, and still more in Rhodesia, that the native African worker must never be at home in a white town, but must always be a temporary stranger whose home was thought of as a distant native reserve. That saved the white employer from having to worry about him (or her) and his housing or other social needs. He was not really there at all except perhaps in the Cape. This idea is still current but becomes more and more demonstrably false. The man who leaves a reserve usually becomes urbanised in the sense that his old surroundings and his old moral order mean less and less. They may well be deliberately discarded, especially by those who see them as completely opposed to progress. But it is not only the moral order which was broken by the towns; it was the pride and confidence which had been part of the old life. And the man or woman in whom all these things are broken becomes lawless, a whore or a *tsotsi;* he no longer has any loyalties; human life, white or African, no longer means anything. He only wants not to be caught. All the more reason why white legislators want to bundle him back to the reserve. But he has been ground in the terrible mills and nothing will make him into a man again.

In the early decades of the twentieth century, some 10% of the Afrikaner population were 'poor whites'. Some had no land, but even those with a little farm did not necessarily have what was called a wall house; their house might be made of poles and mats; they would have no furniture, no books; their children would have no education. Their riches, as with the Khoikhoi and Nguni, whom they had superseded, were flocks and herds. After the first World War a number of them were carefully settled on better land (which had once been grazed or cultivated by—whom?) and expensively nursed into decent farming techniques. Had the African farm workers been given this kind of chance, or had they even been able to earn reasonable wages, they might at least have joined the ranks of small farmers. But this would have threatened the doctrine of *baasskap*. It could not be allowed to happen. Politics were directed towards stopping it.

Yet basic economics stopped it still more firmly. The population on the reserves increased, and the number of cattle; but not the grazing nor the arable land. As erosion grew worse and land fertility dropped, there was bitter criticism of Kaffir ways of farming and living. But the fewer people the reserves could feed, the more had to come out of them looking for jobs and thereby keeping down wages. So the situation for *baasskap* remained satisfactory for the *baas*. To make it more so, an old-fashioned attitude in the reserves was encouraged, with increased powers to chiefs, who, however, found themselves increasingly tied to a white government which gave them salaries and privileges, so long as they did its work and supported its attitude. They became less dependent on the support of their own tribal councils and, in general, on public opinion. A more directly feudal attitude tended to develop, though the basis might be lent-out cattle rather than land. These chiefs realised that they must discourage an independent attitude among their tribesmen and that, although primary education might be allowed, it must not go too far. This means that most educated and politically conscious Africans grow up to hate the chiefs and the chiefdoms, even though many of them came from royal families. But all the more credit to the comparatively few chiefs who have broken through this and led their people in political protest and economic progress—and sometimes to their own personal ruin.

Yet this is not all the story. We must also remember that the Afrikaners were themselves underdogs. The comfortably-off whites in South Africa were mostly British and also to some extent incoming people of other races, many of them Jewish—people who were expert at dealing with money and saw the chance of new money power in this new country. New mines were opened, new industries started, often with outside capital and profits leaving the country. And as the twentieth century went on the Afrikaners forgot nothing that had been done to them, God's people, and apportioned the blame. This surprised the British who felt that they had made liberal settlements, that all should have been forgiven and forgotten. But of course, that is not the way things happen. The British have a habit of bossing people around, all for their good perhaps, and not noticing when feelings have been hurt irreparably. However, this has now been forcibly brought to their notice and they are getting rather better about it.

But the Afrikaners hungered for their little old independent republics which they idealised. They turned their backs on what the present could give them; they refused to forget concentration camps during the Boer War and British attitudes of superiority before and since. They knew that their language had never produced great literature; they knew that they had no artists or (at that time) scientists. But they were determined to be themselves, never to be swallowed. Gradually they evolved the double doctrine of *apartheid* against the British and against the Africans, only modified by a gradual joining up in the doctrine of *baasskap* against the non-whites.

The theory of separate development for all the various races in South Africa had something to be said for it. Each of the conquered African nations was to have a country of its own where it could develop in its own way and its own pace. But if there are ten million Africans and three million whites, it would seem that the land should be divided proportionally or nearly so. Naturally, this was out of the question! Also there was the problem of the Coloureds, not to speak of the Indians. Besides, if the land had been divided in such a way that the new African countries were viable, where would the low paid labour come from, the labour for farms, factories, domestic service and any job beneath the dignity of a white? So, even if the theoretical basis was perhaps sound, it rapidly degenerated into a modern version of the old tribal reserve.

But the Afrikaners themselves hammered their own evolving culture into an image which became increasingly distant from that of the rest of the world. They formed a *bruderbond,* a secret society for cementing Afrikanerdom. They insisted on their own version of any kind of organisation and ended up with an attitude which stopped them from seeing certain unescapable truths.

Here then we leave South African history at the beginning of the political, economic and social patterns which have developed over the last fifty years and with the lines of what would happen next already fairly clear. Even then a few people saw that they were heading for disaster and tried to stop them. But it was like a man trying to stop a moving train. Their names, African, European or Afrikaner, are remembered and honoured even when it is dangerous to speak them in public places. Theirs is another chapter still to be written.

Eighteen

Towards Independence

What makes a country? How is it that only fifty years ago, nobody inside or outside Africa thought in terms of independent African states, and even the oldest, Ethiopia, was almost overwhelmed? How is it that in most parts of Africa white rule, whether aiming at permanent domination and ownership of natural resources and the means of production, or aiming at very distant African self-government, was accepted? Yet now almost the whole of northern, western, eastern and central Africa, consists of independent states.

Probably the present boundaries of these states are not permanent but may be altered as soon as a calmer political atmosphere prevails, although the longer this is put off, the more vested political and power interests arise and the more difficult it will be. But how could these be the right ones, when they are almost always the old boundaries of the colonial powers and often have nothing to do with ethnic or language groups? Yet perhaps national boundaries do not represent the kind of social and political organisation which is best for mankind. They may be out of date. In Europe, for example, thinking people are increasingly critical of nationalism. Old boundaries are being dissolved. Economic and social agreements, especially the Common Market, cut right across them. Can we, in the second half of the twentieth century, think in terms smaller than the whole world?

It is as well to consider what brought into existence the idea of nationalism which has been the force behind the creation of these new African states. This is an area where words are used with very inaccurate meanings, rather as weapons than as means of communication. It is our duty as students of history to do better than this, even though accuracy is less of a pleasure than oratory.

A hundred years ago, there were only a few large, like-minded communities in Africa which could naturally turn into states, apart from the Mediterranean countries and Ethiopia. There were a few big cities in northern and western Africa, including the trading cities of the Niger delta, and the towns further north,

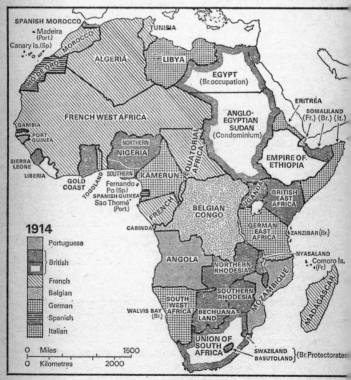

1914

Portuguese
British
French
Belgian
German
Spanish
Italian

0   Miles   1500
0   Kilometres   2000

Map 10

where trade routes met. These had commercial unity and Islam also was the unifying force in some of them. But people's loyalties were overwhelmingly to tribe and kinship groups, often, but not always, organised in villages. What changed this?

One thing was the activity of the Christian missions which broke up specifically African loyalties based on initiation, marriage and death customs and sometimes 'secret' societies. When fragmented people came back, as some Nguni and Sotho peoples did after the *Mfecane,* there was a new pattern of loyalties, sometimes predominantly religious and with European values, sometimes national in the modern sense. But the idea of nationhood came, above all, from European education, starting probably with reading. Perhaps this was thought of first as Bible reading, the story of the Banu Israel who made themselves into a nation. But it turned into the reading of Marx, Lenin, Strachey, Nye Bevan and the rest. Perhaps those who were educated in Church of Scotland missions may have read the Declaration of Arbroath, which is even more explicit.

When people, or their immediate ancestors, have been slaves, the word 'freedom' is very potent. But how did it get tied up with the concept of a nation? There were a good many causes, some of which were more powerful in one country, some in another. Freedom might mean predominantly economic or predominantly political change; it might mean the redistribution of land. It might mean doing away with African rulers who were, or were suspected of being, under the thumb of the old colonial powers.

But once the idea had started among the educated and politically conscious of one country, it moved quickly. Nobody has ever quite been able to quarantine ideas. World War I in which many fine words were blown on the wind, and in which Africans were first involved, though mostly in their own continent, was one influence. Returning African soldiers having successfully killed white men and enjoyed white women, were no longer ready to accept permanent inferiority. It was at the Peace Conference that the first Pan-African ideas began to take shape, under the 1919 leadership of DuBois and Blaise Diagne. Those were the days when Wilson and Lloyd George were talking about the rights of the people to self-determination. Was that intended not to be heard in Africa? The idea of trusteeship, rather than ownership of African territories, was beginning to be taken seriously.

It became apparent to many Africans that the missionaries had not only insisted on a religion, which had meant a tearing apart of their own way of life, but also a general Europeanisation. Much of this, of course, was seized on: the convenient trade goods, the tools and weapons, the medicines, the gadgets, the cheap decoration. It was before the days when Africa became artistic fashion, when the West Coast cloth designed by Africans (perhaps West Indians) and made in Manchester for export, was much sought after by people like myself.

But with this came commercial aspirations, the idea that a man or woman must make money, not for their group, their family or village, but for themselves to spend. This appeared to be part of the Christian idea of the importance of the individual. So did various forms of government, especially voting by ballot. As health conditions improved, more Europeans arrived, Christians of course, but how did they show it? The bitter jibe appeared: 'They told us to shut our eyes and pray. When we opened our eyes the whites had taken our country.' After both World Wars, it seemed more convenient to Great Britain to offer bits of Africa to its returned soldiers and so settle an otherwise embarrassing debt of gratitude. This was responsible for most of the Rhodesian situation, just as the British slump years between 1847 and 1851 were responsible for the organised immigration of fairly poor whites into Natal.

It was only a step on for those bitter Africans to see a universal missionary-government conspiracy. It was seen only too well and horribly in the Congo. When some of the missionaries began to think otherwise about Europeanisation, it was too late for the general picture to change.

Meanwhile African churches began to come into being, churches without whites. In southern Africa, this movement, called Ethiopianism, alarmed the Europeans, both the administrators and also the missions, which in a sense had started off those new manifestations of their religion, which now included such non-white activities as dancing and prophesying. Sanction for all this could of course be found in the Old Testament; but a biblical text can usually be found to prove anything. Such churches shade rapidly into politics. It was said expressly of the National Church of Nigeria: 'all churches exist to serve a given people'. And certainly this thought was behind many of them throughout Africa.

The first political parties were born and the first grievances were put into words and demands, usually very moderate at first. Probably the most general was that there was not enough education, especially secondary, and rising from that, there were not enough opportunities. Enlarge on that, fill in the details, make specific proposals, and you have a nationalist party. The boundaries of your nation are inevitably the administrative boundaries which you can see and feel, though you may well have some relationship with common language and culture groups beyond the boundaries. Yet you and they may have different official languages, as in the Cameroons!

Later grievances were about employment, taxation and above all, the different standards and treatment of Africans and Europeans. Sometimes these became the programmes of explicitly formed political parties or of trade unions. Sometimes they developed out of football clubs, women's or soldiers' associations or anything where people met and talked. It is often only too clear that some insult, perhaps inadvertent, some minor clumsiness even, by a European, desperately hurt some African who could not answer back, given the structure of rule. And this hurt African, who might be better educated and altogether a more sensitive person than the European aggressor, had to take refuge in resentment and hatred. Wounded pride was best assuaged by the sense of being one of a mighty nation whose time would come. This in turn encouraged a Messianic type of religion.

World War II brought allies, not least among the nations who won the war, who were still full of the idealism and courage which had brought them through intense dangers and stresses. But during this war there was the additional possibility, especially in north Africa, of insulting behaviour from an army of occupation, perhaps under great strain, towards an African population which did not necessarily share the same loyalties. New friends or apparent friends got into touch. The pace of African history quickened, although for many it was still not quick enough. But the United Nations type of idealist thought and change made a real difference. Brotherhood began to seem genuine.

After twenty years, trusteeship had affected both Africans and white administrators. All, or almost all, the colonialist powers, to their credit, spent a great deal of money on universities and technical institutes, including teaching hospitals designed on the most modern lines, and vast schemes of disease and pest control. Some of this was no doubt angled so as to create a good relationship between the new states and the old colonial power. This would pay off in the economic field, but some of it was genuinely done in a spirit of scientific altruism. It may be that the same money spent more widely on less showy schemes, more appropriate higher education, and involving more Africans, might have been better in the long run, but this was not clear at the time. Both Great Britain and France have also helped less obtrusively with loans, advisers, the subsidising of new industries or crops, as for instance, in Chad, part of old French Equatorial Africa. One may call this neo-colonialism, but there was not always much alternative for the receiving country and the aid was often given in a genuinely brotherly spirit with the intention of giving as much value as possible to the old colony and perhaps also from a sense of shame at what had or had not been done at an earlier time. Other countries also began to help.

Probably the critical moment for African independence, primarily in west Africa, but also elsewhere, was in 1950. This was the date when the findings of the Watson Commission on the Gold Coast were accepted by the Labour Government in England. I quote: 'The Constitution and Government of a country must be so re-shaped as to give every African of ability an opportunity to help to govern the country so as not only to gain political experience, but also to experience political power.' That was definite.

But not for white settlers who were doing well or hoped to do well or who were doing badly but blamed it on the natives. Wherever there were settlers there was a struggle, often dividing the settlers themselves into the reasonable and the unreasonable. Even when there were few or no settlers the leaders of the nationalist movement could scarcely avoid law breaking if they were going to be acceptable to their own party; the 'prison graduate' status could be useful. Where settlers were really dug in, whether the landlords of the Kenya Highlands or the smaller vine-growers in Algeria, violence was inevitable. As news to the outer world, only European deaths counted. We are only now getting at the truth.

It is most unfortunate that so many people can only be persuaded by direct and unescapable violence, but it appears, historically, to be so. Non-violence worked in the Indian situation because those against whom it was directed were already half willing to be converted : because, on a religious plane, deep spoke to deep, Gandhi to Halifax, Nehru to Mountbatten. In Kenya, Maumau was needed. In Algeria the murders and tortures by both sides, especially the French, were much worse than in Kenya. A great deal of forgiving and forgetting and mutual understanding, based, in southern Africa at least, on the concept of the return of the moral order, will be needed. The end is not yet.

Only the very stupid blamed Maumau or for that matter Poquo on Communism. The imaginary agitator from outside was not needed. 'Communism' is used now as an emotive word. I shall only say one thing about this. When there is a class structure in which the workers—the proletariat—are all black, any white who happens to drop into this category being quickly rescued, and where any black who tries to get out of it is immediately squashed (except for a tiny minority of, say, sportsmen or writers who can be accepted as show pieces or thrown out) then you have a classic situation, and can expect the inevitable development. Outside influence is irrelevant.

But not all African countries have had to go through the phase of violence in order to dislodge the colonialists, or, when they have, it is past history. Sometimes these phases have resulted in valuable friendships and understandings between African leaders and the whites who were on their side or, sometimes, the whites who jailed them. But the transition has been increasingly peaceful. This has sometimes had the rather unfortunate result of acceptance by the newly independent country of rather too much from the old rulers, including elaborate and not always appropriate political systems and the civil servants who are able to work them.

The myth of nationalism has taken shape. To some extent it is the same myth everywhere, needing great names, heroes and martyrs. The idea came from Europe, but it was two-edged. As it grew, much of what was European was pushed overboard, though not, of course, solid things like mines, railways, buses and telegraphs and in general what made those who were in power more powerful. But from the cultural point of view, the nationalists were so anxious to build up the confidence and pride without which people cannot act in a genuinely moral and civilised way, that they had to make speeches, write and sing in terms of hatred of the oppressors which some of them knew to be highly exaggerated and which are often not part of their private viewpoint. They exaggerate or even make up history, not merely choosing different facts or showing the same facts from another angle as I myself have done in this book. All this has brought a certain reaction from whites including those who could have been friendly and useful. A certain amount of friction and injustice is inevitable. Yet the completely just society does not exist and would be intensely boring if it did. What one hopes for is continual adjustment and liveliness.

Meanwhile nationalism has brought a splendid and flourishing flowering of the arts, though this is partly due to the sudden admiration in the art capitals, Paris, New York, London and Edinburgh, for African traditional sculpture and dance, which seems to connect with some part of the European subconscious which has been asleep for a long time. The west coast was first in the field with novels, plays and poetry, some in English and French, others in various African languages which, although never so used in earlier periods, turn out to be highly suitable for everything except probably science. I myself find it extremely exciting that President Senghor of Senegal is, alone of world rulers, a very considerable poet, better, it seems, than Chairman Mao, the other contender. His poems are in French, but are of such a high quality that they come through almost equally in English translation.

It is in the west coast, too, that the tradition of sculpture went easily into modern themes, though there has been a sad tendency to lose the impressive domestic mud and wall sculpture in some countries. It is from here that most of the dancing which so enthralled Europe, came originally. Sodeiba Keita is a poet, a superb dancer and singer, who created the first of the ballet troupes which lit up a whole new area of musical and visual response in other countries. There are several major art centres in other parts of Africa, especially Makere and among the Chagga people. Rhodesia (Zimbabwe) and Zambia are producing some fine painting and sculpture. The art and literature of Africans in the Republic tends to be rather a special case, but in its context it can be intelligent, highly sophisticated and moving by any standards. Some countries have not yet contributed, including my own Botswana. Sometimes this may be due to missions cutting at the roots of the traditional art forms and completely failing to encourage what was there. It was also due to the Africans themselves, who, in an aesthetic vacuum, took to the rags of European culture just as the womenfolk took to the rags their mistresses discarded, though sometimes, as with the Herero, this has built up into a genuine national costume. But, among too many otherwise intelligent southern Africans, anything from Johannesburg is thought to be supremely o.k. Few Africans have realised that, apart from a few dissident homes, Johannesburg and still more the other Boer towns, are not culturally civilised, however efficient they may be technologically. This unfortunate copying of a bad copy has destroyed African values. Or has it? I think perhaps not. The broken branch will grow if the rains come.

With this artistic upwelling there is a tendency to take to (even to invent) a national dress, much to the enrichment of world assemblies, and also to discard mission names. It remains to be seen whether there are any completely different African values, wholly unshared by other people. For myself, I doubt it. I think these are all human values which may have been suppressed in northern and western cultures but which can and will necessarily be drawn out, not from Africans only, but from all of us if ever we can get to the time when mankind is a sum of all its values. Meanwhile, on some things, Africa can give a lead.

What sort of lead? I hope I have given some idea of what this may be in the arts. But the main thing is an African revaluation of some of the main Euro-American concepts which have landed us in our present mess, especially that of the supremacy of money power. In order to make this highly necessary revaluation, the African moral order, about which I have perhaps been boringly insistent, will have to be looked at again and fully thought out, by Africans. It may have to be adapted to deal with the apparently essential large scale of certain economic, industrial and scientific processes. But the countries which are using these processes now are not very good at keeping them in control and Africans who merely copy Euro-American methods and morals are going to be that much less good at disguising them and will sooner or later be hated and despised by their own people. A new look is due and Africa is the most probable source.

There is one other essential place where Africa can give a lead. It is the only part of the world where there is still a reasonable relationship between town and country, though that may not last for long. But it is clear that the wisest of the African statesmen have realised that all progress must be based on the countryside and that large towns destroy values quicker than they can produce new ones. This battle is lost in Europe, North America and India. Africa may be wise enough to win it.

One can write with some confidence of the arts and of the cultural side of nationalism. Here the line of history, of actual facts, even though they may also be a matter of aesthetic judgement, is clear. It is not yet clear in recent economics and history. This is the reason why I am stopping this book on the historical and economic side just before the most recent period, which is the period of the coming into being of the independent African states. There comes a moment when history stops and modern politics begin. Every historian must decide for himself when that is. Some people may feel I have gone too far already in the direction of politics. But it is clear that the nearer one gets to one's own time, the more facts are distorted and can be concealed. Most of us by now, if we have been politically active, must be aware that we often failed to see facts which were under our noses, just because we didn't want to. They would have gone against things we wanted to believe in. And again, something which one sees oneself or with which one has direct connection, outweighs something not seen. Even when it comes to essential written material, there is far more evidence than anyone with limited time can get through.

In modern times some facts are still partly hidden. Others evoke such passionate feeling that nobody can assess them accurately or sensibly. Then the historian's job ceases. Nobody can tell for certain which of these conflicting facts are relevant, which are, so to speak, in the clear line of history. And as documentation piles up, the historian cannot take in everything; the facts which are left out far outweigh those which are put in. Even as it is, perhaps I have gone too far into modern times.

But it certainly does not appear to me that the events in the new African states immediately before and after independence, are yet history. When facts are still unclear, it is wrong to base history on political and economic guesswork. For example, in the field of large scale government, political forms, which may be and usually are called democracy, are beginning to emerge. Some are very unlike those which are called democracy in the west, or for that matter in the communist countries or in India. We cannot say yet which will survive. When a change of government takes place, not because of a different political philosophy but because people have become so angry and frustrated with an existing government that they have to end it, we cannot see its direction. Forcible overthrows are usually of this kind; they mean a change of personnel but not a change of attitude. It is too soon to say.

Again, anything which one may write about orientations towards other African states, even short of federation, may be out of date before this book is in print. So may break-ups of existing states. But it is worth remembering that, to quote from Reuter's guide, *The New Africans* 'Between 1960 and 1966 there were major coups or mutinies in fourteen countries—the Congo Democratic Republic, Ethiopia, Togo, Dahomey, Zanzibar, Tanganyika, Uganda, Kenya, Gabon, Burundi, Central African Republic, Upper Volta, Nigeria and Ghana. Men whose names are synonymous with their countries' fights for independence were deposed, exiled or murdered.' Yet even that, published in 1967, is out of date already. This list has grown. Clearly, there will be a long period of settling down and adjustment, about which historical judgements cannot yet be made. Instead of guessing I shall list the dates of independence of the new African states with their political leaders at the moment of going to press.

AFRICAN COUNTRIES AND THEIR LEADERS

Liberia July 1847 (founded by America). President William Tubman.

Egypt 1944 (British troops remained until 1952). President Gamal Abdul Nasser.

Libya December 1951 (from Italy). Prime Minister Mahmoud Soliman al Maghrabi.

Sudan January 1956 (former British-Egyptian condominium). Major-General Jaafar al Numeiry.

Tunisia March 1956 (from France). President Habib Bourguiba.

Morocco March 1956 (from France and Spain). King Hassan II.

Ghana March 1957 (from UK). Dr. Kofi Busia.

Guinea October 1958 (from France). President Sékou Touré.

Cameroun January 1960 (from French and British trusteeship). President Ahmadou Ahidjo.

Togo April 1960 (from French and British trusteeship). Colonel Eyadema.

Malagasy June 1960 (from France, but still within French community). President Philibert Tsiranana.

Congo Democratic Republic—Kinshasa June 1960 (from Belgium). President Joseph Mobutu.

Somalia July 1960 (from British Protectorate and Italian trusteeship). General Mohammed Ogal.

Dahomey August 1960 (from France). Colonel Maurice Kouandete.

Niger August 1960 (from France). President Hamani Diori.

Upper Volta August 1960 (from France). President Sungoule Lamizana.

Ivory Coast August 1960 (from France). President Félix Houphouet-Boigny.

Chad August 1960 (from France). President François Tombalbaye.

Central African Republic August 1960 (from France). Colonel Jean Bedel Bokassa.

Congo Republic—Brazzaville August 1960 (from France). President Massamba Debat.

Gabon August 1960 (from France). President Albert Bernard Bongo.

Senegal August 1960 (from France). President Léopold Senghor.

Mali September 1960 (from France). Prime Minister Yoro Diakité.

Nigeria October 1960 (from UK). The Federal Government (headed by General Gowon) reestablished its control over the territory of Biafra in January, 1970.

Mauritania November 1960 (from France). President Moktar Ould Daddah.

Sierra Leone April 1961 (from UK). Prime Minister Siaka Stevens.

Tanzania December 1961 (from UK). President Julius Nyerere.

Algeria July 1962 (from France). President Colonel Houari Boumédienne.

Rwanda July 1962 (from Belgian trusteeship). President Gregoire Kayibanda.

Burundi July 1962 (from Belgian trusteeship). Colonel Michel Micombero.

Uganda October 1962 (from UK). President Milton Obote.

Kenya December 1963 (from UK). President Jomo Kenyatta.

Malawi July 1964 (from UK). President H. Kamuzu Banda.

Zambia October 1964 (from UK). President Kenneth Kaunda.

Gambia February 1965 (from UK). President Sir Dawda Kairaba Jawara.

Botswana September 1966 (from UK High Commission Territory status). President Sir Seretse Khama.

Lesotho October 1966 (from British High Commission Territory status). Prime Minister Jonathan Leabua.

Swaziland September 1968. King Sobhuza.

Nineteen

'For a' that and a' that'

'For a' that and a' that,
It's coming yet for a' that,
That man to man, the world o'er,
Shall brothers be for a' that.'

I try to add a few hopes and a little foresight, since all writers should be partly prophets. I look round at my friends here in Mochudi, my fellow citizens of the Commonwealth, and I have to ask myself whether the Commonwealth is anything but a name. This is a hard and painful question. Sometimes one is deeply ashamed that an idea which some people at least worked so hard for, has been so twisted. I admit at once that the Commonwealth, in its early years, acted in a thoroughly colonialist way, only taking seriously the old white Dominions which had the same high standards of living and which had the same commercial policy. Africa was there to be exploited. In those years, membership of the Commonwealth did not help the African countries whose primary producers were at the mercy of world market prices, themselves juggled for money-power reasons; hard work put into increasing output might only result in a lower price. British interests were predominant, just as French interests were predominant in all the old French colonial possessions in the west coast, whose independence was far from giving them economic freedom.

Again, membership of the Commonwealth usually meant, for African countries, the acceptance of a Westminster model constitution. Successive governments in Great Britain assumed that this was always correct. But I believe it is not too late to think again. London is no longer the centre of the world, though it still spends far too much time thinking it is. Yet, if the Commonwealth can rid itself of pressure from the money makers and think in terms of the awful gap between the have and the have-not countries, there is still much that can be done, although essentially Africa must develop itself. What will it be?

Clearly it is not in the sphere of government and order. In so far as the developed countries can help (and inevitably interfere with) the under-developed, this should be through the various international bodies. Now that the Afro-Asians can outvote the rest at the United Nations, the NATO countries may be expected to play it down; it has served their turn. But there are other international agencies and bodies which could be extremely useful, especially if they could stop playing politics to the detriment of their real usefulness and if they would always make sure that their self-styled experts know something beyond their own subjects. We are a long way, I am afraid, from the idea of an international peace-keeping army. Doubtless it makes sense, but too many powerful people are making money out of other people's wars. The risks of peace to money-power appear to outweigh the risks of war to the world.

But apart from the international agencies, the people of the old United Kingdom can do something, as also their cousins in the old Dominions, not least the already non-racial New Zealand. Economic aid brings the question of strings. It tends to be the aid which appears sensible and profitable to the donor country, and that is not always the same as the aid which would really help the African country to develop in its own way, especially with a fairly quick up-grading of rural life and use of improved (but not necessarily expensive) agricultural techniques. It is possible that countries which have gone through this stage themselves could be more use as advisors and helpers than countries which have raised their standard of living entirely by industrial processes.

However, in so far as the Commonwealth can usefully produce aid, terms should be (and over the last few years increasingly have been) as easy as possible, including interest free loans. This may help to bridge the terrible gap. But I am not thinking only, or mainly, of economic aid. I suggest that the people of Great Britain can produce ideas and history and methods of evaluation.

They can say, this is how we came to evolve our parliamentary
system, our particular pattern of democracy; it may not suit
people with a different history, but have a look at it. Alter it as
much as you like; build on your own foundations. Or again:
this is what the Greeks did. That is what the Saxons did. Scots
like myself can say; we made this and that mistake over our
clan lands and organisation; you can easily avoid these mistakes.
Africans, looking at these same bits of history, may analyse them

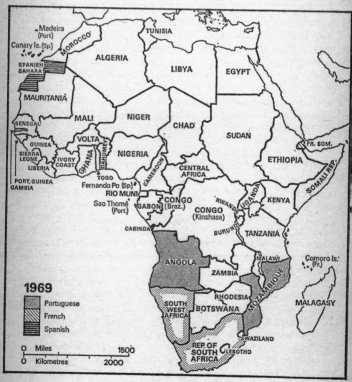

Map 11

differently and add to the sum of critical knowledge. And again the British may be able to learn a great deal, if they will make the effort to do so, from the African pattern of social order and morality. Indeed it is hard not to foresee a time when Great Britain is by no means the most important member of the Commonwealth and will have to do quite a lot of adjusting. A grandmother who can't do this will find she is no longer loved or visited and that is sad for everyone.

Membership of the Commonwealth does not matter so much in the sphere of public and animal health and education. These are better looked after by such bodies as WHO and UNESCO or would be if those bodies were less interested in jobs for the boys and able to do more of what their best people know they should do. But the old UK which is yet humming with people who have both ideals and practice, is continually contributing men and women and ideas to the international bodies. And they go more happily to Commonwealth countries. This is partly language, but partly something less tangible; one knows it when one gets there. The developing countries are already beginning to make their own contribution. The older civilisations, India and Ceylon, have already done so in a big way. There are some exciting ideas and practical methods coming in from Africa over the last few years. There are thought-provoking schemes for children of immigrants who have come to Great Britain, but do not, largely owing to bloody-mindedness by a British minority, feel at home, to go as representatives of VSO to other Commonwealth countries which need their skills and may be friendlier. They will be missed. Meanwhile the Medical Research Council occupies itself greatly with Commonwealth problems. More and more Commonwealth students come to Great Britain, to Canada, Australia and elsewhere, and make friends. I hope and believe that this almost invisible contact makes it easier for us to be friends and understand each other as we must in this world of increasing mobility.

Perhaps the real point of the Commonwealth is that it makes it slightly less difficult for people to love one another. That wasn't true of the old British Empire, of course; it excluded more people than it included. Obviously people don't love one another by being told to; all that is possible is to make the kind of conditions where it can happen. If, as I believe, the Commonwealth can do that, even in a small way, it is worth having and we can be proud of belonging to it. It creates the possibility of contact between rich and poor and the growth of understanding and social conscience. We can also disagree with one another—even violently—and yet not break off relations, or, if we do, they can be mended again, as in a family.

Much of what I have been writing here will be equally true for France and her former colonies and dependencies. The idea of the French Community was far too tied up with political strings to last as such, but political structures are much less important than personal relationships. These I am sure have survived and will grow. And there will be areas where commonsense will surely suggest a way out of the muddle of old European-made boundaries. I think particularly of Senegal and the Gambia, where an old imperialist boundary makes nonsense, but has created awkward status points; but there are plenty of others.

Intermarriage can of course help, but those who decide for it will need courage, intelligence and awareness, much more than at present goes into most marriages between members of the same race. Yet hybrid vigour is one of the important biological concepts. Up to now social pressures have been such that it has rarely allowed itself to show. Today it can be set free. Here it may well be that on the European side the French and the Scandinavians could be socially ahead of the British.

It is apparent from this that I do not agree with the complete neo-colonialist thesis as put forward by many left-wing nationalists. There certainly has been and is economic neo-colonialism, some of which perhaps cannot be avoided during the transition period before the present African states can train their own skilled workers and become self-supporting, but has meant far too many profits leaving a country before it has had time to form its own policies, and there is cultural neo-colonialism which I particularly dislike because it destroys people's own history in their own minds. But I think there is a great deal of exaggeration and the use of neo-colonialism as an excuse to hide one's own genuine defects. Many politicians use neo-colonialism to cover every activity of the older colonial powers whatever its real motive. I may be wrong but I cannot think that the activities of some of the non-colonial (at any rate as regards Africa) powers are necessarily any more helpful. However, an idea such as this is a very useful piece of critical apparatus and should be sensibly used now and in the future.

But the future is not easy. African states are trying out various kinds of government based on different European models; these are being modified in various ways, depending a good deal on how many educated and responsible people there are in any state —or rather what the proportion of them is—and how much respect for order and honesty there is. It is not altogether easy to find the kind of government which is most suitable, especially in poor countries where being in the government is the most lucrative job there is. It is like pushing through thick bush, not able to see ahead, and at present what is usually reported in European countries from Africa is, as Tom Mboya said: 'the blood on the scratches'. In Africa itself we see the advances, sometimes slow, and the process of clearing the bush.

It is surely important that Africans should not simply take, as a matter of course, the form of government which was convenient to those who ruled them and to the civil servants who have been left behind. Africa must build on its own moral basis. From Europe and America, and for that matter from Asia, Africans must take not only technical knowledge, but the ability to look at things calmly and scientifically. Unless they do that, they will never really be able to cope with their own problems and their difficult natural surroundings. They will be able to provide, out of their own past history, courage and patience, and the ability to laugh at things going wrong, even while one is putting them right. They must look at the arts of other countries, including writing and achitecture, but never copy them for copying's sake. They have plenty of their own which only needs freeing and developing. Above all, they must not suppose that the moral ideas of these other continents, including those embodied in their legal systems, are necessarily superior.

What else can the historian see? The areas of immediate conflict are only too clear. It does not look as if some of them could be solved without the use of violence of some kind. Other methods have been tried and failed. Pan-Africanism is clear. It takes various forms and it is not necessarily those who shout about

it loudest who feel it most deeply and who have the most sensible
ideas. Federations, economic and customs unions, unification of
currency and so on make sense, and political jealousies should
not be allowed to stand in the way. Co-operative development
makes sense, since it is a continuation of African clan or tribal
feeling without the exclusiveness or feudal overtones. Boundaries
which were made recently by alien conquerors do not make
sense, yet war is not the way to alter them.

And this problem of black and white which looms so large at
the moment? I can't help wondering whether, after all, it is so
very important. Perhaps in another hundred years it will seem
as out of date and incomprehensible as the feelings people had
about one another during the European wars of religion. I try to
think about the future of Botswana, my own second country. It
is late in becoming independent but perhaps that may mean that
those who are governing it may be able to look about them and
learn from the mistakes of others.

For the first time ever, we live in a very rich world. There is
money enough to do all that we need to help us in Botswana to
bring water which will make our land fertile, to build schools
where we can learn to think for ourselves, to solve our health
problems. It is only a question of priority; the moon or the poorest
countries of Africa? Do we have to pretend to be 'aligned' in
alien quarrels in order to get this money? It seems silly. Of course
I am over simplifying the power situation. But so many people
have been tangling it in webs of complexities that over-simplifica-
tion does no harm.

But money alone, money from outside, whatever its source,
will not solve our problems. All the great African leaders know
this. They know that Africans must help themselves, out of confidence in their own abilities, not an over-weening pride, but a
steady certainty that they can tackle things their own way; that
they can be unselfish, not vain, not greedy, ready to turn their
minds and their hands to any kind of work. It is in the hope of
helping with this that I have written this book. The countries of
Africa must come together, even if a few politicians have to step
down and some civil servants become redundant or accept lower
salaries. They must not allow a gap to develop between town and
country; it could be as dangerous as the gap between haves and

have nots. And it is the country people who are most likely to keep the real African values safe and honoured.

And for my own small country of Botswana, I hope above all that the people will choose to think of ways of developing which will by-pass the greed of the adventurers and the cruelty and selfishness of unchecked free enterprise; this may mean thinking of some new kind of land tenure which will enable go-ahead farmers to get together and produce all that the land is capable of, but which will not allow land grabbing by the rich or land fragmentation by the poor. A plain imitation of European land tenure will not do this, but I trust that Botswana will be wise enough not to imitate the sillier and least genuinely civilised things in white cultures. I hope there will be increasing development of local industries, sufficient labour incentive to absorb the people who may be thrown out from more efficient agriculture; and I hope these will be financed by the people of Botswana, through co-operatives and group savings, so that we shall no longer be a labour pool for richer neighbours. If these industries are spread through the various tribal capitals, as well as other centres which I hope to see in new development areas all over the country, it will be good for everyone.

Above all I hope that our development will be based, not on the ambitious individual, but on the bigger unit: the tribe developed into a unit of agricultural and social progress, but keeping the old concepts of classlessness. But these units within one loved country—and that in turn in good relations with Zambia and our other African neighbours—will be in peaceful and joyous rivalry with one another, with games and singing and dancing, with painting and poetry, beautiful weaving and design. Nobody must go hungry or thirsty; there must be shoes and clothes and books for those who want them, children not conceived ignorantly but only when they are wanted. We must have healthy beasts as our main resource, but varied crops and fruits wherever we can get irrigation. There must be a place for the original-minded, with time to talk and think and make things for one's pleasure, but without the dreadful boredoms, expensive pleasures and consequent crime of the over-rich societies. I hope that in Botswana, everyone's first thought will be, what can I do for my fellow men and women? And I also hope, because we shall have so much to give to the rest of the world, above all to those who are morally dissatisfied with their own kind of society, that Botswana will not be an exclusively African country.

If that is so, let there be marrying and mixing of peoples, with no talk or thought of one being superior to the other. It will not happen at once; noon does not immediately follow daybreak. Perhaps the first generation to think in this way will be among the children I have taught and played with. Or perhaps it will be their children. If I have helped it to happen, may I be one of the ancestors.

FURTHER READING

If you have been interested in this book, you will probably want to follow it up. It is important to read books which give various points of view and to get detailed history out of the many books which, I expect you will find, have been written about the particular part of Africa which interests you most.

If you have the chance, the great thing is to wander round the shelves of a good library pulling out volumes of old letters and diaries, volumes of learned and sometimes not so learned journals, accounts by anthropologists, naturalists, missionaries, hunters or traders. You will find novels and plays which are based on fact, many by African writers, such as Achebe, Soyinka, Camara Laye from the west coast, or Samkange (who comes very close to history) from southern central Africa. Every year there are more young African writers. I believe Zambia will contribute some good ones over the next few years. Kenya and Uganda with writers like Ngugi, who rely very much on the history behind recent events, are important. In the more oppressed parts of Africa sometimes what you get is the gasp of a desperate poet like a fish in a sudden rise. There are also some excellent novels based on fact by Europeans and Americans, such as those of Esther Warner.

You should read some of the history books whose bias you know you will distrust—but please ask yourself why! You will notice that many of them are in flat contradiction with some parts of my own book. I hope you will end with criticism of some of my book at least, based on further facts. But remember, I couldn't put in everything! Yet, if you have read widely, sometimes just dipping in, sometimes reading every word and making notes, you will have gone through an imaginative experience, which will help you to know Africa and, if you are an African, to know yourself.

I am only going to name a very few of the books which I have myself read, during the five years when I was writing this history. Many new books on Africa are coming out. For instance, the first volume of the *Oxford History of South Africa* is now available. This volume goes up to 1870 and is essential for an understanding of the South African problems; it should be in every school library. Volume II will be out shortly. The *Oxford History of East Africa* has been superseding earlier histories.

On the general picture the Penguin *History of Africa* is in print again. *Africa Since 1800* by Oliver and Atmore (Cambridge University Press) is, I think, essential and has an excellent bibliography of fairly recent times. Fage's *Atlas of African History* (Edward Arnold) is very helpful. For pleasure reading nothing beats Basil Davidson's big *Africa* (Weidenfeld and Nicholson) with its gorgeous pictures; you will probably go on to some of his other books. The Penguin Africa series are usually good, but sometimes go out of date rather quickly. Several reputable publishers do African series but, like the Penguins, mostly on current events, though often with a historical background.

As they come out, I have used and much enjoyed the Ibadan History Series edited by Dr. K. Onukwa Dike. These are not only west African, but cover other parts as well. Three books which, though not strictly history, have background and understanding, have specially interested me: *False Start in Africa* by Rene Dumont (Deutsch), *Muntu* by Janheinz Jahn and *African La Philosophie Bantu* by Fr. Tempels. Perhaps here I should also mention the published speeches and writings of Julius Nyerere and Kenneth Kaunda's *A Humanist in Africa* (Longmans). In both, the historical foundations stand firm under today's policies.

Teachers who are tackling African history should get *Africa in the Nineteenth and Twentieth Centuries* edited by Anene and Brown (Nelson) and follow up whichever of the teaching suggestions are relevant to their own areas. This, again, has a large bibliography. A rather less demanding teachers' book, with more pictures, is *The Growth of African Civilisation: History of West Africa 1000-1800* by Basil Davidson with F. K. Buah and Prof. Ajayi, but this is only the west coast. A good upper school level book is *The Making of Modern Africa* by Omer Cooper, Ayandele, Afigbo and Gavin (Longmans). There are a number of history books about northern Africa, many highly controversial, including Fanon's *The Wretched of the Earth* (MacGibbon and Kee).

You will find an increasing number of books with studies of particular problems by authors with special knowledge. Among these I would recommend *The Zambesian Past* edited by Stokes and Brown (Manchester University Press). In reading these newer books you will notice that there are more and more African names among the contributors, as African students begin to explore the histories of their own countries, as only people with the same language and culture background can do. You may also feel that in this book of mine the emphasis may be wrong or that I have made a mistaken choice from the available facts; I do realise quite well that when I have written about European impact on Africa I have written more about the British impact because I can't help knowing more about it. What this means is that history is a living subject, not, as some people say, a dead one, and that one must always be prepared to reinterpret and to admit that one has made mistakes, as I am sure that I, in common with others, must have done. I hope also that the detailed studies which have been coming out in book form will encourage some of my African readers to get information—and write it down at once before they forget!—from those who know the fascinating detail of African history but still keep it as oral tradition. The future will thank them.

THE END

INDEX